A LEICESTERSHIRE
Life

Kenneth Pritchett

**Grosvenor House
Publishing Limited**

Kenneth Pritchett is hereby identified as author of this
work in accordance with Section 77 of the Copyright, Designs
and Patents Act 1988

The book cover picture is copyright to Kenneth Pritchett

This book is published by
Grosvenor House Publishing Ltd
28-30 High Street, Guildford, Surrey, GU1 3EL.
www.grosvenorhousepublishing.co.uk

A CIP record for this book
is available from the British Library

ISBN 978-1-78148-792-1

For Neil

Illustrations by Ruth Pritchett

Contents

Chapter	1	My first day	1
Chapter	2	The firm & a unique office	7
Chapter	3	The finished cattle section & sheep walking	22
Chapter	4	The mart and marriage	29
Chapter	5	Sheep auction, bookkeeping & change	38
Chapter	6	Miss Norman's sale & Ministry sales	55
Chapter	7	On the move at work and home	65
Chapter	8	Cattle market bidding	73
Chapter	9	Pranks, luck money & lairage	84
Chapter	10	Woolsheets & rent collecting	101
Chapter	11	Dealers, escapes, Sam & sheets	107
Chapter	12	Land drainage surveys	123
Chapter	13	White Hart & VAT	144
Chapter	14	Articled students	155

Introduction

I have put together a collection of anecdotes from my forty seven years with Shouler & Son, a firm of agricultural auctioneers, surveyors and estate agents. Two of my former colleagues, Cecil Muse (Curly) and Alan Brown each completed fifty years with the firm. Apart from the three chapters about the 'White Hart', students, and surveying, the chapters are vaguely in chronological order. Much the same as in my working life, where situations changed from day to day, so the book takes a similar ramble from story to story with the occasional glimpse into my private life.

For most of the characters in the book real names have been used, with only four pseudonyms. The book has been written so that my grandchildren have some idea of the kind of working life I experienced, but I hope that you will find these true tales interesting and a few as humorous as I did at the time.

CHAPTER ONE

My first day

Boiling glue and raking ash,
Round the town I have to dash.
Taking letters here and there,
There is no time to stand and stare.
Lick these stamps, ink that pad!
What a start for this young lad!

I stood on a huge, dust laden, coco doormat in front of the office counter. Len Hewes, the office manager, peered at me over the top of his spectacles.

'Go and get him two smocks, Stabby,' he said to the stocky clerk standing beside him. I was horrified. I had only been wearing long trousers for three years, and now they wanted to dress me in a smock on my first day at work. I knew what smocks were. They were coarse linen, ankle length garments, which looked like women's frocks. They were worn by country yokels for farm work, and the wearers were usually depicted in illustrations chewing on a piece of straw. Were they going to give me a pitchfork and a porkpie hat too? My first inclination was to turn and run out of the office, but I didn't. Smocks may have been worn in 1750 but not 1950. It couldn't be possible. Nobody wore such things nowadays, did they? I hoped not.

Len Hewes screwed up his nose, and peered at me again over his spectacles. He looked me slowly up and down as though he disapproved of my appearance. He turned to the clerk, 'Make sure you get them plenty big enough for him, Stabby; then you can show him one or two jobs.'

Stabby ran his fingers through his prematurely thinning hair. He couldn't have been more than five or six years older than me. A big grin spread slowly across his five o'clock shadowed features. He had obviously noticed my anguish over the smocks. Thrusting his hands deep into his trouser pockets, he turned on his heel.

'Follow me, Ken,' he said, 'I'll show you a smock.' With some trepidation, I followed him into Len Hewes' office, which seemed also to serve as the staff tearoom and cloakroom. From a cupboard in the corner, he produced a freshly laundered white smock. To my immense relief, it proved to be nothing more fearsome than a warehouse coat.

Four paces from Len Hewes' office was the door to the cellar, which housed the coal fired central heating boiler.

'Mind how you go,' said Stabby, as we picked our way down the steps. Old boots, raincoats, smocks, and lumber threatened our every step. Stabby paused to tap out a Player from a twenty pack, lit it between cupped hands, inhaled deeply, flicked the dead match onto a pile of ashes, and allowed the smoke to filter from his nostrils as he spoke.

'Every summer this cellar is flooded. The water is always about six inches deep when we come to bale it out. The staff forms a chain up these steps, and we bucket the water out to the drain in the back yard. Only then can we light the boiler.' He paused again and drew deeply on his Player.

I had been listening intently, wondering why we had come down the cellar and what it held in store for me.

'It will be one of your jobs to look after the boiler through the winter, and I'm going to show you how to go on,' he said.

'Right,' I said, glancing round the cellar. It looked foreboding. Large iron fire tools hung on the walls like medieval torture implements in a dungeon. The boiler was huge, and reminded me of a railway engine without cab or wheels. I was to be the fireman.

Stabby took a last drag on his Player before despatching the butt to the pile of ashes. Picking up a shovel, he pointed to the underside of a manhole cover above our heads.

'The coalman tips the bags of coal through there, and half of it has to be shovelled over to the other side of the cellar,' he said, gesturing with his shovel. With one deft flick of his wrists, he opened the fire door to the boiler with his shovel. The heat from the glowing coals enveloped us as he demonstrated the techniques of spreading the coal and prising and removing clinker from between the fire bars. As I stood in the glow of the fire, I knew I wouldn't mind this job.

'There's just one more thing,' said Stabby when he had finished his demonstration,

'At some time Len will accuse you of peeing on the clinker.' He grinned as he waited for my reaction.

'Peeing on the clinker? What do you mean?' I asked.

Stabby chuckled. 'Len gets a bee in his bonnet about the horrible smell which drifts up through the grating in the back yard, and he swears that it's caused by someone peeing on the hot clinker. It's only the acrid smell of the clinker but he won't be convinced. Don't worry about it though, he's been saying it for years.' I thought he was pulling my leg, but he wasn't.

Our next port of call was the saleroom adjoining the office. Access from the office was across a small, enclosed, back yard. Four galvanised dustbins stood against the office wall, their lids balanced precariously on top of the protruding rubbish. Old wooden sale boards were stacked against the saleroom wall. At one end of the yard was an outhouse with one door and one window. As we crossed the yard Stabby was lighting yet another Player. He stopped and nodded towards the outhouse.

'That's the back kitchen, where we boil the kettle for the tea, and where you'll boil the glue.'

I didn't question him about this job. I guessed he would be showing me later. Instead, I peered in through the open door. Apart from the small window, the only light provided was from a gas mantle. The word kitchen was a misnomer. A more appropriate title would have been junk room. Concealed within the murky depths were boots and wellingtons which had obviously been used in the cattle market. There were old clothes, sale boards, a roll of binder twine, a scythe, brushes, buckets, mops and bric-a-brac of all descriptions. The only semblance of a kitchen was provided by the low stone sink and single gas ring at the end of a flexible pipe. The interior was so grimy that even the hunk of soap in the sink looked in need of a good wash.

'How do you ever find anything in there?' I asked.

'Ah,' he replied,' the kitchen has been waiting for you to arrive. No doubt Len will get you to clean it out before long.'

The saleroom or mart, as it was always called by the staff, was almost empty.

'This is a big place,' I said, trying hard to make some contribution to the conversation.

'It won't look so big when we've crammed seven hundred lots of furniture in here. You'll spend a lot of time in here - we all do,' said Stabby, 'That's one of the reasons you need a smock.' He pointed towards two large sliding doors, secured by a heavy brass hook and eye. 'That's where we unload all the furniture.'

We walked across the mart. The floorboards were rough and uneven, worn by years of trundling furniture to and fro. Stopping underneath two large trapdoors in the ceiling, he looked up. The two doors were open upwards. A single wheel pulley was suspended from a beam above the trapdoors, and on the end of the heavy rope a single iron hook was attached.

'The room up there is known as the wool room,' said Stabby, 'Mainly because all the wool sheets are kept in it, but we also store furniture up there, and that is pulled up on the rope, so I hope you're strong.'

'Hmm... I see what you mean,' I said, eying up the pulley. Fresh from school mathematics, I could see at a glance that the effort required to pull up any item of furniture would be more than the weight of the load on the hook, and it obviously took two people to pull up a heavy item, with a third person to receive it upstairs. As I looked at the pulley, there was something puzzling me.

'How do you hook the furniture to pull it up, Stabby?' I enquired, intrigued by the thought of a large wardrobe dangling precariously on the end of the hook.

'Ah, well!' he replied, 'we wrap the rope around the furniture, and slip the hook back over the rope again. If we don't find the exact point of balance, we end up with a load of firewood on the floor.' He paused, and added wistfully, 'Just make sure you're not standing underneath.'

Stabby glanced at his watch. 'Good grief, it's half past nine already. I must get off on my rent round. I'll show you how to boil the glue, and do the paint, later on today. No doubt Len will find you plenty to do in the meantime.'

As I made my way back to Len's office, I reflected upon that first half hour. I had to keep the boiler stoked up, boil the glue, and do the paint, whatever that entailed. I had been given a brief insight into the labour involved in the mart. I had been set on as an office boy cum clerk, but where was the clerical work? The rest of that first day passed all too quickly. I replenished the inkwells, laid out fresh sheets of blotting paper, re-conditioned a pile of envelopes from the morning mail, learnt how to do the glue and the paint, stamped and took the post, and delivered all the local area mail on my bike.

Before I left the office that evening, Len Hewes gave me a key to the office door, and a piece of advice.

'Now then, my lad, do as I do. Get a chain, put your keys on one end and fasten the other end to the top of your trousers. If you lose your keys - you lose your trousers!' he said with a smirk. Having seen Len, the following day, standing on tiptoes, because his chain was not quite long enough, struggling to insert his key in the lock, I decided not to take his advice. The thought crossed my mind that, if someone suddenly opened the door from inside whilst his key was firmly embedded in the lock, he would be caught off balance, and dangle from his chain like a puppet on a string.

CHAPTER TWO

The firm and a unique office

Learning more about the job.
How to make an extra bob.
Lift this dresser, sweep the floor,
Finish that, then back for more!
Maybe, one day, I'll make the grade,
Like plans of mice and men are laid!

Shouler & Son, a family business of agricultural auctioneers, surveyors and estate agents, was established in Melton Mowbray in 1846, and it was Mr William Shouler, who, on Saturday September 27th 1862, held a special sale, at Elgin Lodge, of the oil paintings, engravings, and hunting sketches for the trustees of the late John Ferneley, Melton's noted artist. This created, within the firm, a precedent for auction sales on Saturdays, which has always been a bone of contention with a few members of staff, who liked to play or watch sport on a Saturday afternoon. Saturday sales, however, have always proved popular with the public.

It appeared to me that the office furniture had changed little since Mr William's time. The centrepiece of the main office on the ground floor was a large mahogany extending dining table, around which some of the clerks sat. In one corner of the office stood three, heavy, metal safes. Alongside these, set against the wall, was an elaborately carved parlour cupboard. Occasional tables, brass letter scales, stationery cases, gunmetal inkstands and many other items of antiquity were in everyday use. Some clerks sat on "Smoker's Bow" armchairs. The partners' offices were furnished with antique desks, glazed bookcases, and side tables.

Clients, waiting in reception, were not so well provided for, and sat on plain wooden chairs with no upholstery. They were also in constant danger from the large pile of "Farmer's Weekly" magazines which sat on the counter above their heads, leaning perilously towards the client who was seated closest, and threatening to spill over at any second.

There were three partners in the firm, Fred Shouler and his two sons, Arthur and Malcolm. Fred was semi-retired and came in occasionally to help with the books. There were two senior employees who were chartered auctioneers, Sid Wheeldon and Eric Pacey.

The lower echelons comprised Len Hewes, the office manager, four male clerks, Cecil (Curly) Muse, Alan Brown, Jack Ravenscroft, and Reg Stapleford (Stabby). There were three female secretaries, Pearl Burton, Eileen Davison, and Jean Carter. These ladies also had the roles of cashiers on sale days. I was the new office boy and, to complete the staff, there was an articled student, John Sail, who was a tall, strong young man, who frequently walked around with his shirt tail poking out from the waistband of his trousers. His morning tea break was never complete without a couple of cream buns from Beaver's cake shop across the street from the office. John lived at the "Ferryboat Inn" in Stoke Bardolph, Nottinghamshire, and came to work on a powerful, blue, twin cylinder, Douglas motorcycle. He took me for a ride on it one day. He raced up Scalford road for half a mile, slewed round, then zoomed back again with me clinging to him in desperation. It would have been more comfortable had there been a pillion seat, but I was sitting on the mud guard. That was my one and only ride on that machine.

The old wartime team spirit was still in evidence within the office, with staff interchanging jobs when necessary, and, whenever there was a sudden heavy workload, everyone pitched in to help.

The cattle market has always been held weekly on a Tuesday. Every Monday it was my job, as office boy, to close all the gates to the sheep and cattle pens ready for use the following day. I also had to sweep out the small market office and replenish the paint in the pots used in the store cattle auction. There were four colours used. The paint was ordinary household paint, which I fetched from the local ironmonger's shop, Leonard Gill's, in the town. The oil was poured off the top of each tin of paint before use.

My first Monday in the market was most revealing. The abattoir stood only a few yards from the market office, and its double wooden doors were wide open. As I swept out the office I could see all the activity within the abattoir. Never before had I given much thought to the origins of the meat on my dinner plate, but now all was revealed in stark reality. I knew instantly that I could never work in such a place. I was even more horrified later to see two of the slaughter men, arms and aprons heavily bloodstained, standing outside in the sunshine, tucking into their sandwiches with some relish. How could they enjoy those sandwiches? I wondered.

I came to the conclusion that they treated the situation much the same as an oil-spattered car mechanic would do - it was just a job.

After the office had been cleaned, I gathered up all the empty glue pots and carried them back to the main office in readiness for the 'boil up'.

The glue, used for sticking lot tickets to the backs of cattle and calves, arrived from the manufacturers in large drums. (These, too, were kept in the back kitchen.) It was of a thick consistency rather like toffee. A hunk of glue was extracted from the drum and placed in a large iron saucepan. It was then heated on the gas ring in the back kitchen until it thinned and became easier to spread. If the end result was too thick, I was in trouble with Len Hewes, and in even more trouble if it was too thin.

To prevent the back yard becoming a human "flypaper", the glue was poured into the pots on an old sale board, about four feet square, and kept solely for this purpose. Due to constant spillage, the board had become extremely tacky, and, when not in use, was propped, face inwards, against the wall in the yard.

Late one December afternoon, I had just finished pouring the glue into the pots, when I heard the upstairs toilet window open. I glanced up and was just able to avoid a handful of water cast in my direction.

'Ken, I want you to come and help me with some beast trays in the market,' said Stabby, grinning, as another handful of water cascaded down. 'I'll be down in a couple of minutes.'

I grabbed the glue pots and joined Stabby at the front door. We walked to the cattle market, which was conveniently situated about fifty yards from the office.

Beast trays were rough, heavy, wooden structures, similar to field gates, but much heavier and taller. They were used, generally, for making extra pens to hold cattle, and were tied together with ropes. It took about half an hour to drag the trays into position, and we were fortunate to walk away with no splinters in our hands.

It was almost dark as we walked back to the main office. As we reached the front door we could hear a commotion inside. I could hear the agitated voice of Len Hewes.

'Where's that boy?' he shouted, 'I'll give him what for when I find him.'

I peeped through the window of the swing door, and saw Len Hewes holding a shoe aloft for the staff to see. 'Oh! no!' I gasped, 'I left the glue board on the floor of the back yard, and Len Hewes has walked on it in the dark.'

His ten year old leather shoes, his pride and joy, were in a mess, and so was I. Glancing at Stabby for inspiration, and finding nothing but amusement on his face, I decided that discretion was the better part of valour, and beat a hasty retreat, returning only when I was sure the storm had abated.

Although I have referred to the office manager as 'Len Hewes', it was impressed upon the office staff that he should always be addressed as 'Mr Hewes', and so he was. Even the partners addressed him as 'Mr Hewes'. The Shouler family partners were addressed as 'Mr Fred,' 'Mr Arthur,' and 'Mr Mac'. It was common practice, however, to refer to all people by their initials, so the query 'Is AWS in?' was often heard around the office. Len Hewes's office was in a strategic position. From his desk behind the door, which was invariably open, he could peer round the door to see all persons entering the office, hear all telephone calls at the main switchboard, which was just outside his office door, and hear most of the activity in the main office. He would let off steam by handing out imaginary punishments to people after particularly acrimonious encounters. I heard him on two such occasions. After one clash with an irate woman at the counter, he returned to his office muttering 'All women should be strangled at birth.' It was obvious that the woman had won the day.

On the second occasion, when referring to workers on strike, he said, 'If I had my way, I'd put 'em all in a concentration camp.'

His office was also the focal point of the ground floor. Here the staff hung their coats and smocks. Here the tea was brewed in a large teapot and poured into the cups, some to be taken round the office, others to be drunk in situ by staff or partners ready to leave the office or just returning from jobs. Here the dirty smocks were changed, and bundled up along with towels ready for the laundry collection. Here it was also that many little tales about the events of the day were recounted over those "cuppas" by returning staff and partners.

Mr Mac strode into Len's office just as Jean was pouring the tea into cups on the tray.

'Oh! great! I am just ready for a good strong cup of tea,' said Mr Mac, tossing his valuation book onto the table adjoining Len's desk and flopping onto a chair in the corner.

'Had a good day Mac?' asked Arthur who had returned a few minutes earlier, and now stood near Len's desk sipping his tea.

'No I have not' said Mr Mac, emphatically,' I have been to do the stocktaking for the Wilson brothers, and I got rather more than I expected.'

'What happened Mac?' asked Arthur, raising his eyebrows in surprise.

'Well, we had finished the valuation of the livestock and all the outside inspections, and I had just sat down in the kitchen with the two brothers. We were just going through the tenantright invoices, when up jumped that loony sister of theirs and punched me right in the mouth, muttering something about me not being fit to lick my father's boots. God, she fair made my teeth rattle, and, to add insult to injury, the brothers sat there laughing. I still don't know what she was muttering about, but I've told the brothers that I'm not going back until they've had her locked up.'

'You've had quite an afternoon Mac,' said Arthur, trying hard to conceal a grin behind his teacup.

It was from this unique office, and the vantage point it provided, that Len could see when Mr Croll arrived.

Len dealt with most salesmen almost before they had set foot inside the office, giving most of them short shrift, but not Mr Croll.

Mr Croll, who supplied most of the stationery supplies for the office, was not typical of the pushing, smooth tongued salesman who usually invaded the office reception area. He was a small, dapper, polite and quietly spoken man. Always smartly dressed and wearing a homburg, he would be around the same age as Len. Whenever he arrived, Len would greet him with a handshake, and they would sit in Len's office, where Mr Croll would be given a cup of tea and they would find lots to talk about. Why Mr Croll received this red carpet treatment, I could never understand, because the products he delivered appeared to be no better than merchandise from any other firm, but he was the only salesman to be 'honoured' in this way.

It was in Len's office, too, that all the sale sheets, together with carbon copies of the invoices and vendor accounts, were stored in a pigeon holed stand. This only added to the hustle and bustle already occasioned by the tearoom, cloakroom, and laundry facilities. As if this wasn't enough, the office cleaner, Mrs Avery, kept some of her cleaning polishes in the cupboard. It was an office which had a strange, magnetic effect on all and sundry. Reg Shouler, Mr Fred's brother, who was a bachelor and a retired bank manager, lived close by in Park Road, and called in most mornings to sit in this office, where he studied his Financial Times, sipped a free cup of tea, and smoked a cigarette carefully extracted from a small leather case. He would leave the office when the pubs opened and hobble down the street to the "men only" bar at the Half Moon. Here he sipped his half of bitter before returning home to join his two spinster sisters for lunch.

The firm's books were balanced every six months after the 30th June and the 31st December. In the weeks following the two dates, Len would extract all the relevant figures, whilst a member of staff, usually Stabby or I, entered the details into balancing notebooks. Len had a unique balancing procedure, but effective nevertheless. There was no mention of debtors or creditors, but headings would read "Due to the firm," or "Due from the firm." The books had to balance exactly and no stone was left unturned until they did. One year, Stabby and I sat for two weeks checking off all bank payments and receipts looking for a one shilling discrepancy. It would not happen nowadays, but it was important then – more a matter of pride.

'Grab your smock, Ken, Jock's here with a load,' shouted Curly, the senior clerk. Curly, in his early thirties, and with fair hair true to nickname, kept the office books. Six years previously he had been Sergeant Cecil Muse, and had been mentioned in despatches whilst serving in Italy during the war. Now his uniform was a white smock, and we were waiting for Jock Ewart to open the doors of his furniture van. This was a familiar cry in the office, and unloading and lotting up furniture became part of my daily routine. Most members of staff participated to some degree in the preparation of the sales, but it was Curly, Stabby and I who carried out the bulk of the work. The mode of transport, for large items of furniture or house clearances, had only recently changed from Horace Bland's horse and dray to Jock Ewart's furniture van.

Jock, in his late thirties, had been a feted, local boxer in his youth, and the alignment of his nose and ears bore testament to that fact. He once showed me a boxing poster, which depicted him as "Battling Jock Ewart." His huge hands, which had delivered many an uppercut, now lifted heavy furniture with consummate ease. He was an easy-going individual, spending more time chatting to people than his business could really afford, and his knowledge of the latest local gossip and intrigue was unsurpassed. Jock's raucous voice, which still bore traces of his northern origins, could often be heard teasing some hapless woman as she passed by on the other side of the street, or arguing with a policeman who had dared to suggest that he should move his van. Norman Street was extremely narrow just outside the mart, and, even though the van was parked half way across the pavement, traffic jams occurred on a regular basis.

I took a liking to Jock the first time I met him.

'Grab hold of this sideboard, Kenny,' he shouted. He had already discovered my name, and Kenny it was from that day on. Very few people called me Kenny. I jumped up onto the tailboard of his van and helped to carry the sideboard into the mart.

'How do you like your first job then?' asked Jock.

'Oh all right so far, Jock, but this is only my first week.'

'Ah, but wait till you're selling like Curly and Alan, you'll enjoy it then,' he said, as we lowered the sideboard into position in the row.

The thought of me becoming an auctioneer had not entered my head before. I thought I had an office job. I didn't even realise that Curly and Alan sold. I thought that only qualified auctioneers were allowed to sell. Now the first seeds were sown, but it was to be some years before harvest.

Three months had elapsed, and I thought that I was really getting the hang of the intricacies of the terminology and procedure in the mart. I could reasonably sort the wheat from the chaff. All the antiques and better modern items of furniture were lotted for the afternoon sale, commencing with lot 301. Items of a lower quality, kitchenware, feather beds, crockery, books, bicycles, washing machines and so on were numbered 1 to 300, and sold in the morning. We sold the proverbial kitchen sink on many occasions. It was usually the case, however, that many late entries were included. These would be given numbers, like 300A and 300B. Often we ended up with

350 lots or more in the morning sale. Many times we used the whole alphabet on extra lots - we rarely turned away custom, after all, it was the vendor who paid the commission.

I was now conversant with the common abbreviations used in the booking book, R.S. for rush seated, L.B. for ladder backed, C.S. for cane seated, D.L. for drop leaf, M.T for marble topped and so on. I knew the difference between reserves and commissions, and the meaning of "bought in" and "trotting". I had also learnt how to pack a hundred wooden chairs into a compact stack by interlocking the legs, and how to sweep the dusty wooden floor with a two feet wide brush, after first sprinkling the floor with a solution of Jeyes fluid and water, administered by flicking with a hand brush.

There was one thing, however, which puzzled me. The first task, on the day following a furniture sale, was to look through the sale sheets, and note all the lots which had been "bought in" (failed to reach their reserve prices.) These items were then re-lotted for the next sale.

'Stabby!' I shouted, one Friday morning, as I perused the sale sheets of the previous day's sale, 'there's something a bit odd here. Two lots owned by a chap called Singleton of Stathern were bought in, but there's no reserve price on the sheets.'

'That's all right,' replied Stabby, as he trundled an easy chair into position, 'people sometimes bid for their own stuff to help the price along, and if they get too greedy, they often get it back.'

'Oh I see,' I said, turning over the sheets, 'This chap Jacques, of Harby, must be a real glutton then - he's got half a dozen lots not sold.'

Stabby looked a shade uneasy. He paused from his work, leant his stocky frame over the back of an easy chair and wistfully blew a cloud of smoke into the shaft of sunlight streaming through a mart window. After a brief deliberation he spoke,

'Well, it's not quite that simple. Look, Jean will be in with a cup of tea in a minute, why don't you nip across the road and fetch a couple of packets of crisps, and I'll tell you more about it when we have a break.'

It was always a luxurious moment for me to sink into the softest and most comfortable armchair in the mart, and enjoy a packet of Smith's crisps whilst sipping my morning tea. Even the act of un-twisting the small, blue packet of salt, and sprinkling it over the crisps, was, somehow, pleasurable. Stabby, too, seemed to be savouring the moment as well as the crisps, as he lolled back in his chair. He carefully examined the curvature of a large crisp before popping it into his mouth. After a moment's reflection, he spoke. 'Those two names you picked out from the sheets are fictitious - what we call non-de-plumes. The furniture actually belongs to the boys.'

'The boys?' I queried.

'Yes - me, Curly, Alan and Jack. The rest of the staff always refer to us as "The Boys". We buy and sell a few lots of furniture in the furniture sales, and share out any profit at Christmas. We use non-de-plumes so that other people are a little more in the dark.' He drained his cup, screwed up his empty crisp packet and flung it towards me, 'Come on,' he said, 'let's get the rest of this furniture drawn out.'

It soon became apparent that I, too, needed to supplement my wage of two pounds per week. I hoped "The Boys" would allow me to join their enterprise. I did ask, but, after two or three refusals, I retreated to lick my wounds. My ego had been dented, but not for long.

After a while, I decided that I would do a little trading myself. At the next furniture sale I bought an old tea trolley for two shillings. Painstakingly, I repaired a loose joint and gave the trolley a coat of shining varnish. Imitating the tactics of "The Boys", I lotted the trolley for the next sale, using a non-de-plume, one Mr Frisby.

Whilst the sale was in progress, it was my task to find and identify each lot from the huge stack of furniture behind the rostrum, so that the porters could carry them forward for sale. When, at last, my lot was placed on the rostrum, I felt a surge of adrenalin inside. This was a totally new experience for me. Would I make a profit? Had it been worthwhile? I didn't have long to wait. The trolley was quickly sold for one pound five shillings. I had made over one pound profit - half a week's wage! I felt like a millionaire. Encouraged by my initial success, I soon discovered the benefits of Topps' scratch cover polish, Brasso, elbow grease, and a little ingenuity. Ironing boards and dining chairs could be recovered, furniture dusted and polished, boxes of glassware washed and re-arranged - anything to make a profit in the next sale. I didn't make a profit on every lot, but, overall, it was a handy supplement to my wage.

In succeeding years, as other juniors started work with the firm, I joined forces with each of them in turn, and continued the enterprise. "The Boys" now had ongoing competition. One of my partners was Graham Watts, and on one occasion we attended a village jumble sale some fifteen miles away, and bought a car load of household items. On the return journey, the car was so loaded that items protruded from the boot and windows.

The goods were offered in the next sale, where nearly every item made a good profit. Graham and I walked around like Cheshire cats for some time after that sale.

With another of my partners, it was decided to test the long held belief that many people do not know the value of lots they buy in the mart. We bought, from Woolworths, several items which we considered we could re-sell at a profit in the mart. Among these items were three cased socket sets, priced around one pound each. When sold in the following sale they produced a handsome fifty per cent profit. The belief had been well founded. Furthermore, unlike other vendors, we paid no commission on our sales.

Periodically, on a market day, a dealer would arrive at the cattle market in his lorry with a load of household items, which he had bought in bulk as "seconds" from Freemans, the mail order company. These would be lotted and sold around the air raid shelter in the paddock behind the cattle market, where all sundries were sold. Our small trading concern would buy several ironing boards to resell in future furniture sales, and usually made a decent profit.

CHAPTER THREE

The finished cattle section & sheep walking

Check those bills, and then this sheet,
Make your figures clear and neat !
I stand inside the fat beast box,
In old clothes and thick grey socks.
Dot those 'i's and cross those 't's
Even when your fingers freeze !

Tuesday in Melton Mowbray has always been market day. It is the day when the streets are packed with stalls and people. Until recent changes, the cattle market resounded to the clanging of hand bells to herald the start of the auctions, the lowing of the cattle, the bleating of sheep, the clatter of descending lorry tailboards, and the shouting of the auctioneers, buyers, and of the vendors as they shouted the praises of their stock. There was always a hustle and bustle and a sense of urgency about the trading within the market. The cattle market had an atmosphere which I consider was unique and had to be experienced to be properly appreciated.

For the auctioneers, market day was always the most important day of the week. All other work was suspended on Tuesdays. Our main office in the town closed until the completion of the cattle market activities in late afternoon. Lunch breaks were non-existent. It was paramount that the market books were balanced before staff finished for the day. Sometimes it was late evening before this was achieved, and on such occasions sustenance was provided by the firm, usually in the form of cream cakes from Beaver's bakery across the street.

Wellingtons or boots, waterproof leggings, old clothes and a white smock were the standard items of clothing for clerks in the sheep and cattle auctions.

For the eighteen months before my conscription into the army for National Service, I was assigned to work alongside Len Hewes in the finished cattle section. In 1950 the wartime meat allocation system was still in operation, and butchers could not buy their fatstock at auction. Instead, farmers entered their animals fourteen days prior to the intended day of allocation. This knowledge then enabled the Government to allocate specific numbers of animals to towns around the country. It was to be 1954 before fatstock returned to auction.

Farmers were paid a fixed rate for their cattle. This was determined by the weight of the cattle and the grade given to them. There were about ten different grades, ranging from "super special" for the best quality, descending through "special", A+, A, A-, B+, and so on down to grade C. The grades were decided by two Government appointed representatives. One local farmer, Henry Morris, represented the producers and Percy Langton, from Great Glen, represented the butchers. Where agreement could not be reached in any instance, the grade was decided by the mediating grader, Arthur Shouler. Sometimes the disagreements became quite heated, and at such times, Percy would turn his back on Henry, saying, 'I'm just going for a Jimmy Riddle while you cool off, Henry.'

Len Hewes recorded the weights and grades in the grading book, whilst I filled in the delivery note books, one book for each destination of the cattle. On a Tuesday we could deal with 350 cattle, and often we would allocate an "overflow" of 150 on a Saturday morning. Apart from those transported by road, we usually despatched about 100 cattle by rail to London. During late afternoon, these cattle, often including two or three bulls, would be herded from the pens and walked across the rear of the market to the nearby L.N.E.R. station.

One Tuesday, before I joined the firm, during the droving of the beast to the railway station, a lady complained to the police that she had come face to face with a bull on the pavement on Scalford Road. The bulls were over a year old and should have been staffed and led, but it was far easier to run them mixed with the other cattle.

After the police became involved, Arthur Shouler, was prosecuted and taken to court, where he appeared before the local bench of magistrates, which was chaired by a friend of his. Arthur questioned the police sergeant about his ability to know that the bull was over three years old as stated, which left the sergeant in a quandary. After Arthur explained to the magistrates that the number of teeth was the test, the case looked like collapsing. However, the astute police superintendent called Arthur to the witness box, where he was obliged to tell the truth on oath and admit that the bull was over one year old. The chairman was highly delighted and promptly fined him £1.

Some of the cattle would be allocated to Melton, and if there was a particularly nasty tempered bull in for allocation, this, too, would be kept at Melton for safety reasons. The local abattoir's fasting pens were situated only fifty yards away from the fat cattle pens. It was normal to fast beast before slaughter.

One Tuesday we had to deliver a rather bad-tempered, horned Jersey bull to these fasting pens. One drover held a bull staff, which was clipped to the ring in its nose, whilst two more drovers took the strain on a rope haltered behind the bull's horns. There was abundant verbal encouragement as the reluctant bull dug in its front feet, and the two men on the rope heaved to get the bull moving. Suddenly the bull changed its tactics and lunged forward, tossing his head from side to side.

'Hold him! Hold him!' shouted the men on the rope, but the poor man was clinging to the staff in desperation as he was flung about like a rag doll. One moment he was on his knees, the next his feet were six inches off the ground. With one heave of its powerful shoulders, the bull catapulted the man across the road, leaving the staff dangling uselessly. This left the two men at the end of the rope in a precarious position, because it is not possible to push a rope. From the horrified looks on their faces, it was not difficult to predict their next move. They dropped the rope and fled for their lives. Luckily, there were already a few heifers in the fasting pens, and these were quickly released to join the bull. With the bull's attention now focused on the heifers, the drovers were able to deliver all the beast into the fasting pens.

During the winter months, the fat cattle department seemed to be the coldest spot on earth. Oh! to be the dairy cattle clerk, or the calf clerk, who both worked where brick walls and a roof fended off the cold wind and rain. In our department, apart from the pens, there was a salering (but no sales), a weighbridge, a cattle crush and an open fronted wooden shelter, in which Len Hewes and I stood to record the weights and grading details of the cattle. The wind blew directly into the shelter, and the rain lashed in likewise. Although I wore a pair of woollen mittens (gloves were too cumbersome to wear whilst writing,) my fingers usually got so frozen that I could barely hold a pencil. I suspect that Len was quite fed up with my moaning about frozen fingers.

It was a cold day when Hazy met with his accident. Hazy, whose his real name was Hayes, was a casual worker from Nottingham, and was employed to work the cattle guillotine, so called because its action vaguely imitated the notorious method of execution used during the French revolution. When a beast walked into the narrow crush, a metal frame descended over its neck and held it fast while it could be assessed, earmarked, and a grade mark clipped on its back. The frame was operated by pulling down on a vertical, flat and narrow bar with a handle at the lower end. The bar slid down between two protruding metal brackets and secured by slipping a steel pin through a hole in the bar underneath the two brackets.

The whole operation had to be performed at speed because the first instinct of a beast, when it feels the frame touch its neck or shoulders, is to rear upwards to dislodge it. Hazy did not get the pin through the hole quickly enough just once. A beast reared and its powerful shoulders caused the bar to shoot upwards with Hazy still holding the handle, and a protruding bracket sliced off the end of one of his fingers.

It was the first time I had heard a man scream in agony, or seen so much blood. Poor Hazy was rushed to hospital, and was away from work a long time. The guillotine was modified, and I never complained about my frozen fingers again.

During the early 1950's, one local farmer and cattle dealer, William Marriott from Saxby, was still walking a large bunch of cattle through the town to the cattle market on Tuesday mornings. Similarly, we walked in the sheep from the Leicester Road field early on Tuesday mornings.

The field was triangular in shape, and was situated, about half a mile from the cattle market, adjacent to the railway bridge and line. Nowadays it houses a DIY store and car park. During my early years at the firm it was used on Mondays, and on the day preceding a special sheep sale, by farmers and dealers as overnight lairage for sheep intended for sale in the market. Each lot of sheep would be marked in some way by the owner, and the owner's name and marks on the sheep would be recorded in a booking book, which was tied to the field gate for that purpose.

At six o'clock on Tuesday mornings, four clerks would set off from the office to fetch in the sheep. On dark mornings we carried torches to warn approaching traffic. With two men in front and two behind, getting the flock to market should have been an easy task, but, alas, it was rarely the case.

The flock usually consisted of sheep of differing age groups. These ranged from frisky young lambs, always ready to start off at a gallop, to aged, plodding, ewes. Often there would be one or two old ewes with distinct walking disabilities. Quite often these lame pensioners would ride to market in style in the rear seat of Sid Wheeldon's car, which he brought along later for this sole purpose.

It was difficult to maintain a steady walking pace. There would be frequent shouts of 'Hold 'em up in front.' On that short journey to market there were many obstacles to overcome. Apart from private driveways, there were garage forecourts, park entrances, a bus station which was open to the road, several road junctions and a roundabout. The two men in front desperately tried to close all the bolt holes, but we were fortunate if we got the flock to the market without a few trampled flower beds and a chase around a fleet of Barton's buses.

Arthur Shouler also owned a field on Burton Road. This field was always known as the tank field. Occasionally, on a Tuesday morning, we had to walk in sheep from there to the market. Similar obstacles were encountered, and once, in the Market Place, the flock wandered underneath a heavy lorry, which had stopped to allow the flock to pass by, but sadly the lorry moved off with one of the sheep still underneath the lorry. It was a gory sight which met the townsfolk on their way to work, and another job for George Clarkson the local knackerman from Saxby Road. Occasionally, an old ewe would die in the field and, the following day, would be buried in the field by the gravediggers, who were, of course, the flexible male clerks of Shouler & Son.

The traffic on roads through the town was steadily increasing and it was not many more years before the walking of beast and sheep to market was abandoned completely.

CHAPTER FOUR

The mart and marriage

National Service draws quite near.
It's going, going, gone, I fear !
Two years away across the sea
To spend my time in Germany.
Glimpses into private life,
As now I have some trouble and strife

Having spent many of my boyhood summer holidays on a farm, I was already in love with the countryside; so I felt quite at home in the cattle market, working among livestock. By the time I was seventeen, the fascination of the auction world held me in its grasp. Once this happens, it usually lasts a lifetime. Auctions, apart from providing many bargains, can create disappointment and elation in equal measures. They are also responsible for that essential ingredient of life - humour. A woman once told me that she wouldn't miss our monthly furniture sales for all the tea in China.

'Better than going to the cinema.' she said.

My leisure hours were spent playing football for a local village side, Somerby, and cricket for Holwell Works, a large ironworks at Asfordby Hill, two miles from Melton. Here the greatest hazards to the batsmen were not the bowlers, but the sun setting behind the slag bank, and the grit, which constantly found its way into ears and eyes as it was borne on the prevailing wind from the nearby blast furnaces.

Conscription into HM forces loomed ever nearer. Soon I would have to register and undergo a medical examination. My elder brother, Ray, who was already doing his National Service in the Royal Engineers, would soon be demobbed. In the meantime I had a third leisure pursuit - of a girl I had spotted outside the school on Wilton Road whilst walking in the sheep one Tuesday morning.

The park or "play close", as it is called today, was the evening meeting place for many of the town's teenage population in the nineteen fifties, and it was here that I first met the girl. Her name was Margaret, the daughter of a local businessman. She soon became my steady girlfriend and a central part of my life.

On 1st May 1952, I set off to start my National Service. I had said all my fond farewells, and Margaret promised to write to me regularly, a promise which she kept throughout my two years' service. The two years seemed endless, but eventually I found myself, once again, pushing open the swing doors of Shoulers' office.

Nothing appeared to have changed. Jack was still sitting in his usual place at the dining table, poring over the rent accounts. Stabby, with his five o'clock shadow very much in evidence, was lighting a Player. Curly was pulling on his smock, and the cry was still the same.

'Grab your smock, Ken, Jock's here with a load of furniture.'

As we walked together across the back yard, I noticed that the gas mantle light in the back kitchen had been replaced by an electric light. At last things were beginning to change at Shoulers, I thought, but then I noticed the hunk of soap in the old sink - it still looked in need of a good wash.

It didn't take long to get back into the swing of market days, furniture sales and the variety of jobs which filled our working lives.

At that time, the days I enjoyed most were the monthly furniture sale days. Apart from making a little cash on the side, occasionally I got to book alongside the auctioneer. It is here, from the rostrum, that the auctioneer conducts the sale and appears in complete control, but sometimes the unexpected can happen, and sometimes it can prove costly.

The furniture sales were popular and it was often difficult to accommodate everyone in the mart. There were several regulars, who claimed their usual chairs an hour before the sale was due to start. Some would bring flasks of tea and sandwiches whilst others would nip out to "Greasy Joe's", during the lunch break, for fish and chips. Our monthly sale day was a day out for many local people.

It was a wet October Thursday, and it seemed that more people than usual were packed into the mart. All the chairs were occupied, and people sat on cookers and dressing tables, which were on display around the room. They stood on the stairs leading to the toilets, and in the porch and doorways - anywhere to gain a view of the proceedings.

The morning trade was brisk, and good prices were realised. There were a few new faces among the regular buyers.

The new buyers were still present as the afternoon sale commenced. As the sale progressed, one of the new buyers, in particular, was buying a lot of furniture.

'This man, Oswald, has bought a lot of stuff,' whispered Alan to me between lots, 'Do you think he's all right?'

'Perhaps he's won a fortune on the pools,' I replied, jokingly.

'He must be furnishing some flats. He's been a damn good customer,' mused Alan.

We were more than halfway through the afternoon sale before the alarm bells began to ring in Alan's head. 'Do you reckon he's all there?' he muttered from the corner of his mouth. 'Look at the people around him grinning every time he bids.' His worst fears were soon realised. Mr Oswald, who, until now, had appeared quite rational, was reacting to the grinning people around him.

'Woof woof, yap yap,' he barked at them. Just as some dogs will take exception to a postman, so Mr Oswald vented his anger at the grinning people around him. We were dumbfounded. It was an astonishing sight. The sale was halted while the unfortunate Mr Oswald was escorted from the mart. We discovered later that he had a history of mental problems, and was in no position to pay for the lots he had bought. The situation was unprecedented in the firm's history.

At the conclusion of the day's sale, Alan rushed into the office to fetch Mr Oswald's bill. 'Look at all this blooming furniture he's bought,' he groaned, 'We shall lose a fortune on this lot when we re-sell it.'

Because Mr Oswald had bid for so many lots, and because of the presence of other new buyers, there had been a marked increase in prices. His lots were re-sold in the following sale, and the firm lost a substantial amount of money. We were obliged to pay out the vendors of the lots in question at the inflated prices realised in the original sale. It must have been their lucky day - it certainly wasn't ours!

Humour is an essential ingredient of any auction sale. Usually it is provided by the patter of the auctioneer, but occasionally it manifests itself by accident.

The afternoon sale had been in progress for two hours. It was hot and stuffy in the mart. The porters were beginning to tire. Alan was trying hard to keep up the momentum of the sale.

'Come on you chaps. Get a row of stuff lined up ready for showing, and who's carrying back? Look! That chest is still sitting there. Liven your ideas up a bit,' he shouted.

Peter and Les, two of the porters, struggled to carry a large rolled up carpet to the rostrum. They dumped it, unceremoniously, onto the tables, and laughed as clouds of dust billowed out into the audience to mix with the swirls of tobacco smoke, already present. The women seated in the first few rows were well prepared for this nuisance as they clutched handkerchiefs to their faces.

'You dirty devils,' shouted Mrs Keegan from her usual seat near the pillar. The people at the rear of the mart smiled, pleased they were not sitting near the front. Alan was not amused.

'How many times do I have to tell you? Unroll the carpets and get them ready for showing,' he shouted. The carpet was sold and carried away. Peter cursed as his finger was punctured by a tack left in the edge of the carpet.

'Serves you right,' shouted Mrs Keegan.

Jock Ewart's job was to display the lots on the rostrum. He would often amuse some of the audience by parading in a fur stole, or top hat, whenever either was offered for sale, or make some crude comment about a chamber pot or bidet. Jock often incurred Alan's wrath, because he often drifted away from the rostrum, leaving others to display the lots whilst he took orders, at the sliding doors, to deliver items which had just been bought in the sale.

'Jock, Pay attention to your job - you're supposed to be showing the lots,' shouted Alan.

Jock returned to his job just long enough to put the next lot onto the table, but immediately sidled back to the doors. The lot was a pair of log boxes, which had been fashioned by cutting an oak barrel into halves. The cooper, who had so carefully crafted the barrel so many years ago, would not have been too pleased to see the transformation in his end product. Each half had been varnished and brass handles attached.

'There we are,' shouted Alan, 'A pair of nice log boxes. Who'll start me at a tenner? Eight then? Well, it must be six. Thank you madam, at four pounds only bid, at four pounds.' ..... He stopped abruptly. We stared at the boxes. There was a loud creaking noise. One segment of a log box toppled slowly inwards, followed by another, then another. The metal hoops dropped with a clang on to the table, and the whole box collapsed within a few seconds.

When the laughter finally abated, and a semblance of order restored, Alan turned to the porters. 'Put that lot down, chaps, we may be able to offer it again later.'

The demise of the log box was probably due to its weakened state, or was it the hidden hand of the cooper exacting his revenge?

Within months of my release from National Service, Margaret and I were engaged and we were married at St

Mary's Parish Church the following year. Our first home was a small terraced house, No1 Victoria Street. My father in law, Arthur (Skip to his friends) Farrows, who ran his own decorating business, had put in a good word for us, and we were able to rent the house for eleven shillings a week. The landlord, Mr Gregg, lived in a tied cottage. He was gardener to Captain Crosfield, who lived on Burton Road. Mr Gregg had bought the house to move into when he retired, and I only occupied it on a "Gentleman's Agreement".

The only heating in the house was from open fires in grates. There was no electricity upstairs, and my knowledge of DIY was practically non-existent at that time. However, I ran a wire from downstairs to our bedroom and installed a temporary connecting extension socket, so that we could get the benefit of the two bar electric fire, which had been a wedding present from my colleagues at work. Unfortunately, in my ignorance, I had run the wiring from the lighting circuit, and we had hardly got into bed before we could hear a crackling and a distinct smell of burning rubber. My first bit of DIY had been a complete failure, and the fire was promptly disconnected in case the house went up in flames.

In the kitchen stood an old soft water pump adjacent to a low stone sink, but there was a mains cold water tap. There were large holes in the front room floorboards, but this hardly mattered as we couldn't afford to furnish the room anyway. The room was utilised as a garage for my bicycle and also for the pram, when our first son, Neil, was born the following year. A small back yard gave access to an outside toilet and a coal shed, and in one corner of the yard flourished a sweet scented lilac tree, our only bit of vegetation.

It was in this house that our only daughter, Elaine, was born two years later. Shortly after this, Mr Gregg announced his imminent retirement and asked us to leave the property. We moved into a council house in Arden Drive on the other side of town. Although the rent was much higher, we now had the luxury of a bathroom, inside toilet, and a garden. There was also a communal green for the children to play on.

It was during the few years at Arden Drive that my chance to become an auctioneer finally arrived. It had always been traditional, within the firm, that, when a prospective auctioneer was to be given his chance to sell, he would be told only fifteen minutes before the start of the sale. He then had little time to worry about the ordeal ahead. For some unknown reason, I was informed the day before. Although I was excited by the challenge, the prospect of selling in front of a mart full of people was still rather daunting, but it was exactly what I had hoped for.

I slept little that night. The possibility of making a complete hash of everything was uppermost in my mind. What if I missed most of the bids? Would my voice be strong enough to carry to the rear of the mart? We had no microphones in those days. During that long, long night, I went over the introduction to the sale many times, and sold every item of our bedroom furniture in my imagination.

The following morning I arrived early at the office. The sale started at ten o'clock, so I had over an hour to get through before the moment of truth arrived. I tried to appear unconcerned, but I was nervous as I checked the commission lists, and prepared a list of notices to be read out prior to the sale.

At ten o'clock Alan and I climbed onto the rostrum, and took our seats to loud cheers from the porters, and some of the "regulars" in the audience, who had inside information about the initiation about to take place.

Using Alan's gavel, which had long since lost its handle through sheer volume of use, I rapped the table two or three times, and popped a small mint in my mouth to assist the saliva flow. My mouth was still unnaturally dry, and the butterflies were still fluttering as I read out the notices. Once these were completed, it was time for the rules of the auction. These I had heard so often that I could remember every word.

'We sell under the usual conditions of sale - copies hang in the office should anyone wish to read them. The chief ones are cash before removal and all lots at your risk at the fall of the hammer. We have three hundred lots to get through this morning, so please get your bids in quickly and shout up if I don't see you.

There we are, lot one, a box of crockery. Who'll give me two pounds? One then? Thank you madam, at one pound only bid, at one pound, at one pound two shillings...four...six... eight...do I see ten anywhere? ...going then at one pound eight shillings.' Bang! - The hammer was down. I had sold my first lot.

After the first few lots, I began to warm to the task. I didn't miss any bids - there were too many people around, who were only too eager to point them out to a novice auctioneer. On my first appearance I was allowed to sell only one hundred lots. Once these were sold, Alan took over the reins. I still had a lot to learn, but I had made a start. The firm could now call upon the services of another auctioneer.

CHAPTER FIVE

Sheep auction,
book keeping & change

Keeping books and Pay As You Earn.
Lots of skills we have to learn.
Not for us a course at school,
But in at the deep end of the pool.
When the golden eagle flies,
Ten bob will surely be the prize.

After my return from National Service, my job during the next two years, on market days, was penning and booking out the fat pigs, where Curly was the auctioneer. The old wartime allocation system finished in May 1954, and butchers could, once again, buy their fatstock at auction. A section of the sheep pens was used to house all the fat pigs. This was not an ideal situation. The pigs were weighed in bunches on a weighbridge and then penned in the iron railed pens. It was becoming good practice to produce leaner pigs by feeding them meal instead of the swill which was used during the war years. Buyers could identify the odd pen of pigs which had been fed swill simply by the smell of the pigs. Invariably, the meal fed pigs made more money than the swill fed ones.

Pigs from different litters were often in the same pen, divided only by a wooden sheep hurdle (called a tray by us and a flake by others,) which was secured at both ends by two pieces of wire attached to the pen rails. Pigs will invariably fight with pigs from other litters, and the trays proved ineffective against pigs determined to attack their neighbours. Cecil Neal, of Sikes and Smith, and I were continually separating fighting pigs, and re-erecting the trays between the lots. I was pleased when I eventually moved to book the store sheep.

At this time there were three firms of auctioneers in the cattle market, Shouler & Son, Melton Farmers Ltd (A farmers' co-operative,) and Sikes & Smith. Whilst the firms were generally in competition within the store sections, they had joined forces to sell all fatstock, and this amalgamation was called Melton Fatstock Auctions. In later years, auctioneering firms in all regions of the U.K. united to provide competition between markets rather than within markets. Melton's firms became Melton Livestock Auctions, and eventually became known as Melton Mowbray Market.

It was during this time of competition within the market, that I started to work alongside Sid Wheeldon in the store sheep. Sid, in his late fifties, had been with the firm for many years, and had been made a partner, together with Eric Pacey, during my absence in the forces. He was an impatient man and possessed a deep strong voice. He was an excellent tutor in the art of gaining and keeping trade. He led by example, arriving early in the market, and working alongside his drovers, drawing and penning sheep. By doing so, he was there to chat to and advise farmers when they arrived at the market. These were sound principles which ensured a good show of sheep in Shoulers' pens, week after week.

Sid, however, had his failings. He was prone to sudden outbursts of temper, usually of short duration, and sometimes directed at obscure targets.

'Blast the bloody man who made this tray!' he yelled as he stubbed his toe against a wooden sheep hurdle.

'Damn and blast and set fire to it,' as he fumbled with a knot in a length of binder twine. In complete contrast he would "butter up" a client by bestowing upon him a military rank. 'Good morning Colonel, and how are you today?' he would say, beaming from ear to ear.

Waterproof leggings were essential in the sheep auction, but more essential was the first aid box in the market office. The demands on this box were frequent as hands encountered pieces of thorny briar or barbed wire entangled in the fleeces of the sheep.

The pens were open to the elements. Auctioneer and clerk performed a balancing act along a plank fixed above the pens, and just wide enough to accommodate a pair of size ten boots. On a wet and windy day, and with an umbrella stuffed down the front of my smock, I found it difficult just to stay on the plank. Booking out and trying to keep the booking book dry just added to the difficulty. The sheets invariably required drying out in front of the small electric fire in the market office.

Whether it was with the girls in the office or with me in the sheep auction, Sid always had some difficulty with names.

'Pass my flask, Flossie,' he would say to Eileen in the office.

'Rex, grab hold of this tray,' or 'John, help me lift this ewe over the rail,' to me in the pens, but often he would shout 'Boy, are you ready to start?' This was his favourite name when addressing clerks and drovers. This difficulty with names was emphasised even more when he announced that, 'The next pen of lambs is from Edie and Ada Cook of Bourne.' This should have been E.D. and A.D. Cook. There were no ladies in the partnership.

There were nicknames, too, for most of the dealers. There was "Gilly" Fisher, from Welby, whose generous paunch hung over the top rail of the pens. There was "Watty", "Truthful", and "Snowy", a young dealer whose hair was almost white. There were many others, but Sid rued the day he decided to give a nickname to a new buyer in the cull ewe section.

It was a warm September Tuesday, as we were enjoying an Indian summer. The leaves on the trees overlooking the sheep pens were tinged with the first sign of autumn. The sudden rush of breeding theaves and ewes had not yet arrived. The cull ewe section was fairly full, as farmers sold the broken mouthed ewes, which they thought were not worth breeding from again.

Sid leant on the counter in the market office. He stared thoughtfully out of the office window as he finished off his flask of tomato soup, his Tuesday sustenance for the task ahead. He turned abruptly to the girls behind the counter.

'Knocking down paper!' he snapped. Jean hastily rolled up the remnants of an old booking book, which often served this purpose, and handed it to him. 'Come on, boy,' he growled at me, 'It's time we made a start.'

Unlike other auctions in the market, we never used the traditional hand bell to herald the start of the auction. We didn't need one.

'Ewe buyers! Ewe buyers! This way gentlemen,' boomed Sid. His powerful, deep voice could be heard at the far end of the market.

As soon as the preliminaries were over and the sale under way, it was obvious that Sid's spirits were rising as the trade was brisk, and there was a new bidder among the dealers. He was a tall, well- built man, with sandy coloured hair. He was wearing wellingtons, old trousers, and an open necked shirt with the sleeves rolled up to the elbows.

'Do you know him?' whispered Sid between lots.

'Never seen him before,' I replied.

'I reckon he's a dealer,' said Sid, confidently. He had made up his mind.

The new man continued to bid for several pens of ewes, without any success. At this point, Sid decided to give him a nickname.

'You're out, Sandy,' he bawled one minute, 'Have another one, Sandy,' the next. Eventually "Sandy" was successful and bought a pen of ewes.

'What's your name and address, Sandy?' shouted Sid.

The reply came in a voice that would have graced the corridors of Eton or Harrow.

'Captain Spencer, Rotherby,' said "Sandy", with a smile.

Sid turned to me, his mouth agape, 'Oh my Gawd,' he mumbled, 'I thought he was a dealer.'

I had never seen Sid so embarrassed. The captain, to his credit, was obviously enjoying the irony of the situation, and was now grinning broadly. The dealers, as usual, were making a meal of Sid's predicament, and guffawing loudly. It was not the only time, however, that I was to witness Sid's embarrassment.

'Anybody can sell when the trade's good,' is a comment often bandied about in discussions between auctioneers. The point being made is that it takes a good auctioneer to sell anything when there is little demand. If the trade has been exceptionally good - 'We've had a flyer today.' If the trade has been poor - 'I had to take the dealers on a bit today,' or 'It was like trying to get blood out of a stone today.' The main topic of conversation after the auctions was the state of the trade in each auction.

'What do yer mek o' your trade today then, Arthur?' asked one farmer of Arthur Shouler one Tuesday.

'Nobody wants any store cattle, George, there's no grass about. We could do with a week's rain,' replied Arthur.

'Ay, that's right enough, and Alan tells me baby calves is a rum trade just now an' all. He reckons it's all to do wi' stopping this export job. I dunno' what things a' coming to.'

It was on such a Tuesday that we started the culled ewe auction. With his false teeth neatly wrapped up in his handkerchief, and safely stowed away in his trouser pocket, and the preliminaries over, Sid was ready to do "battle" with the dealers. It was soon clear that the trade was several shillings a head down on the previous week's trade. The dealers were "standing in", and would not bid against each other. There was little interest.

'Can you see the devils looking at one another,' snorted Sid. If one thing infuriated Sid more than anything else, it was the practice of "standing in". After a few cheap lots, Sid decided to take the dealers on.

'At seventy two (shillings) only bid… at seventy two…four…six…eight'… He paused, hoping that one of the dealers would bid and break the deadlock, as there had been no genuine bids so far, but there was no response. The dealers looked at each other again.

'Are you in then, Sid?' shouted Gilly, laughing.

Sid was becoming more furious by the second. 'You're trying to pinch the buggers,' he yelled. Beads of perspiration stood out on his brow. He pulled out his handkerchief to mop his brow, forgetting completely about the precious contents. His false teeth shot out and disappeared among the ewes in the pen. Despite the frantic efforts of the drovers to retrieve them, they were smashed under the feet of the milling ewes.

'Talk about broken mouthed ewes,' shouted Watty, 'We'll be selling you soon.'

Sid was not amused, but the misfortunes of others always seemed to amuse the farmers and dealers. I must admit to a little schadenfreude myself at that moment.

Thereafter, Sid's new set of dentures found a safer hiding place in an old tobacco tin, but for several weeks after the event, the dealers teased him mercilessly, and at the start of proceedings each week it was the same chorus, 'Have you put your false teeth away Sid?'

In addition to the weekly sales of sheep and lambs, special sales of breeding sheep and lambs were held every autumn. The sale day began at six a.m. with two gangs of men fetching in the sheep from the two overnight lairage fields. By eight o'clock these sheep had all been drawn, matched and in their correct pens. Pens were allocated prior to the sale and a catalogue of entered sheep was drawn up and printed.

Prizes were awarded for the best pen of ten sheep in each section of theaves, ewes and lambs. There were also prizes for the best rams. Second and third place prizes were also awarded.

When all sheep were penned, it was a rewarding sight, to walk down the alleyways between the pens, and see the pens of Masham and Mule theaves and ewes with the tufts of wool on the tops of their heads marked with a dab of yellow or purple paint, each pen vying with its neighbours to catch the judge's eye. Even more imposing were the pens of Border Leicester ewes with their large, prominent white noses.

When the judging was over, red, blue and yellow prize cards were pinned to the plank above the winners'pens, each card helping to increase the sale price when the sheep were sold.

Even more rewarding, in my view, were the delicious ham sandwiches, carried to the market in two wicker shopping baskets, each basket covered by a freshly laundered teacloth, and accompanied by two steaming hot jugs of coffee. These were prepared at Dakin's café, just outside the market gates, and delivered promptly at ten o'clock to the market office every special sheep sale day. The sandwiches were delicious, and their popularity confirmed by the speed at which they disappeared.

Dakin's café was always full on Tuesdays and sale days. Mrs Dakin provided a basic meat and two veg, followed by a sweet, at a most reasonable price. It was here, after the hurly burly of the market, that farmers could eat and discuss the events of the day.

The café has long since disappeared, making way for all the new development in the town, but, whenever I saw Mrs Dakin in later years during her retirement, I was pleasantly reminded of those days, and I could almost taste, those delicious ham sandwiches and the steaming hot coffee.

My first insight into the world of book-keeping came when Arthur Shouler was asked to run Manor Farm at Langham, near Oakham, for Mrs Emmeline Hugh Smith. Alan Brown kept the books, whilst I paid out the wages for the farm employees and a few estate workers. I now had to find out how to work the P.A.Y.E. system as no tuition was ever available.

It was the task of one of the estate workers, Neddy Williamson, to read the water meter at Ruddles Brewery in Langham every quarter, and log the readings in a book. The water was supplied from a spring on the farm and was used in the production of their popular beers. After receiving the book from Neddy, I would invoice Ruddles for the water used.

During the same period, Alan kept the farm books of Major Norman of Pickwell. Again I calculated and paid the wages.

During subsequent years the firm kept the farm accounts and paid the farm wages for Lord King of Wartnaby. Howard Johnson was the farm manager, and his son Geoff took over the reins when Howard retired, and the popular manager is still there today.

For many years I travelled, fortnightly, to Stoke Rochford, where I paid out the wages for the Stoke Rochford Trust Estate and for Lady Sarah McCorquodale's grooms. At that time the estate agent was Warwick Purchase, a chartered surveyor who worked from an office in the centre of the village. From there, with the assistance of his secretary, Marion Collins, he managed a large estate. Eventually, Shouler & Son were asked to manage the estate, and Warwick became a partner in the firm, but remained at Stoke Rochford to continue the good work. One of the younger partners, Simon Allam, gradually took over the reins at Stoke and Warwick retired a few years later.

For a year or so, I also paid out the staff wages for Mrs Colman of Scalford Hall. She was the widow of Colonel Colman, whose family business produced the condiment which became a household name, and the family reputedly became wealthy more by the amount of mustard left on the side of the plate than was actually consumed.

Mrs Colman had a small farm, but it was not run on a commercial basis. The only sheep on the farm were brown and white Jacobs, presumably for show, in the field in front of the hall. I paid a weekly visit to deliver the wages, where, on most occasions, Mrs Colman's small dog would run out from behind the butler, down the front steps, and try to sink its teeth into my Achilles tendon. Eventually I would be ushered in to see Mrs Colman.

One week, during discussions about wage details, she suddenly paused and looked pensive for a few moments. 'What do you think of the dustmens' strike?' she asked at last.

Taken by surprise, and not wishing to appear to be taking sides, I came up with a rather lukewarm reply.

'I suppose it will be most inconvenient when all the rubbish starts to pile up' I said half- heartedly.

'Well I think the dustmen have a very dirty job and they fully deserve a rise.' she countered.

Giving her support to the striking dustmen was the last thing I expected to hear from Mrs Colman, but I soon discovered how forceful she could be. The late Colonel's financial affairs were in the hands of a leading bank. Thus, whenever Mrs Colman required money, she had to deal with the trustees from the bank. I gathered, from our conversations, that they often received a severe reprimand from her because they would never allow her the amount of cash she required. I know that certain employees at the Inland Revenue and National Insurance offices hated the thought of visiting her. They, too, did not receive the most cordial of welcomes. She would write across the top of letters from these two departments "I do not understand this," and return them.

Arthur Shouler was now the senior partner, and as such he determined the wage structure within the firm. It was common knowledge within the office that he based this structure on the wages paid to building society employees. As a director of the Melton Mowbray Building Society, the acquisition of this information presented little difficulty.

The wages were always reviewed, and any increase initiated, each year, on the first day of July. Should there be any adjustments, a list would be handed, a week or so beforehand, to Curly, who paid out the wages. There was always a certain amount of speculation among the office staff as the due date approached. There was a coded phrase used by the staff to ask Curly if he had received the list.

'Has the Golden Eagle flown, Curly?'

'Yes, we've got half a bar.' would probably be Curly's reply, as ten shillings was usually the amount of the rise,

The fact that Arthur based our wages on Building Society wage rates was always a sore point with the staff. The comparison was like comparing chalk with cheese. At one point the male clerks were so dissatisfied with the level of wages that it was decided that we should seek a meeting with Arthur to complain and put over our point of view. No staff member belonged to any union, so whatever Arthur decided had to be accepted. The only alternative was to seek employment elsewhere. At least Arthur would always listen to our grievances.

At the appointed hour, Curly led the gang of five up the stairs to Arthur's office. At the top of the stairs he turned left and round into the office, closely followed by the others. When we were all seated we found that one member of the deputation was missing. Apparently Stabby, who had been bringing up the rear, instead of turning left and following the others, had marched straight on and into the toilet - a definite case of cold feet.

Arthur was always affable at these meetings, and, although he listened patiently to our grievances, the meetings were not very productive.

The most we ever got out of such a meeting was a promise to look again at the structure. Although our wages were low, there was one consolation. All the staff received a good bonus periodically after a particularly successful sale of surplus stores for the Ministry of Defence.

Most firms of auctioneers used a simple code to protect reserve prices and other sensitive valuation figures from prying eyes. For example a phrase which is easy to remember is used to represent the figures 0 to 9. The one used at Shoulers may still be in use today so I will not disclose it. However, it is simple to coin a similar phrase like "CATS IN LOVE", where C = 0, A = 1 etc. thus a reserve on the book of £ASO would be £137.

The partners used code in the valuation books when they carried out annual stocktakings for farmers. The code was used almost on a daily basis, and soon became so familiar to clerks that adding up in code became as easy as using numerals.

At the time I joined the firm, and for some years after, sales literature and leaflets were produced using a "Banda" machine with a hand operated drum mechanism. The print on the resultant copies was of a purple/violet colour, and, for days after use, the smell of methylated spirit pervaded the atmosphere in the control room, where the Banda was housed. The room was so named because the government meat allocation scheme for the local area was "controlled" from there during the war and for several years after the war was over.

When the first photocopier appeared in the office I was given the rather dubious privilege of operating it. It was housed on top of a large mapping chest on the first floor landing. Bottles of liquid chemicals stood to one side of the machine, and the integral trough at the front of the machine was filled prior to use. A "master" negative was produced and prints were taken, using photographic sheets, from this negative, which were then developed by feeding them through the trough. It was a messy business and my trousers were soon spattered with ugly brown chemical stains.

The evolution of the photocopier was rapid. Previously, copies of plans had to be traced, and copies of letters produced, as they were typed, using carbon paper. Sale particulars could now be produced by the score, and very soon the old Banda machine became obsolete, and disappeared from the scene. The lingering aroma of methylated spirit in the control room gradually disappeared, but was soon to be replaced by a much worse one.

Whilst the partners sat at their antique desks, most of the staff used old tables as makeshift desks, until the day that the local pet food factory, "Petfoods", offered for sale a number of desks in the monthly furniture sale. Two of the desks were bought by the firm and duly installed in the control room upstairs. Alan had one desk and I had the other, and we were pleased that, at last, we had a proper desk each. There was a price to pay, however. As the desks had previously stood for years in a factory which used fish as one of its main ingredients in its cat food, there was a distinctive aroma which again pervaded the atmosphere in the control room, and lasted for several months.

Within the office a most unconventional method of passing on messages was used. Written messages were not left on desks. Instead, they were left at strategic points on the floor and stairs, and held in place with brass scale weights.

Mrs Avery, the office cleaner, was given special instructions for Sid Wheeldon's office, as he insisted on keeping rolled up plans and drawings in his waste paper basket.

One weekly ritual carried out in the office was the proofing of the firm's adverts for the local newspapers, The Melton Times and the Grantham Journal. This was performed by Sid Wheeldon, not from the comfort of his office chair, or other quiet room, but on the main office counter, where he would commandeer most of the counter by spreading out the proofs and getting the first available member of staff to read to him. This made it difficult for other staff to serve customers. The main reason for this choice of venue, I suspect, was to enable him to keep his finger on the pulse of office business.

He did, on a few occasions, break off from his proof reading, and snatch the phone away from a junior member of staff when he thought the call was not being handled to his satisfaction. This was hardly a confidence booster for the staff member involved.

Although his office was situated only a few yards from the counter, Sid would usually conduct interviews with prospective house purchasers at the counter. On some of these occasions, other customers would be waiting to be served. Invariably, his first blunt question would be, 'How much cash have you got laddie?'

Arthur Shouler tried to encourage him to change his ways. 'You really ought to take your clients into your office, Sidney,' he told him on more than one occasion, but to no avail. Sid just could not change his ways.

The wind of change blew only as a gentle breeze at Shoulers in those early days. When adding machines were first introduced into the office on the initiative of the partners, the move was bitterly criticised by Len Hewes.

'All your brains will go rusty, and eventually you will not be able to add up without using a machine,' he would say. There is no doubt that he had a valid argument, but the new machines were here to stay, followed later by pocket calculators.

The toiletries for the office were purchased by the female members of staff, and, they, as most women do, liked to try out new products. When the innovative soft toilet tissue replaced the Izal medicated toilet paper in the only office toilet, it did not make everyone happy. On the morning following its installation there was a rumpus at the top of the stairs. Sid Wheeldon had just made his customary visit to the toilet.

'Who the devil's bought this new toilet paper?' he thundered, 'It's no bloody good. I keep putting my fingers through it.' Despite his protests, the tissue paper was there to stay, and no doubt he fully approved of the advice printed on the new toilet roll holder which read "*£75000 may come your way, but don't sit here and dream all day.*" This referred to the top payout at that time by Littlewoods football pools.

Petty pilfering has always been a thorn in the sides of small businesses, and we had our share, too. Small items would disappear from the mart whilst the furniture sale items were on view to the public. Although members of staff were on duty to keep an eye open for any pilferers, they were difficult to detect.

Harry Howitt, who had worked on Fred Shouler's farm until the farm was sold upon Fred's retirement, was now employed in the mart. Harry was on duty, keeping a watchful eye on the furniture sale items, one viewing day, when he noticed that an item was missing. After an unsuccessful search, he rushed into the office.

'Somebody's pinched the electric razor,' he declared.

Len Hewes, who was standing at the counter, looked up.

'How do you mean? How do you mean?' he asked in an agitated manner. Len often repeated a question when agitated.

'Well it was there one minute and gone the next,' said Harry, resignedly.

'Are you sure it's not been moved somewhere else?'

'I've looked everywhere, and I can't find it,' said Harry.

Len was getting more annoyed by the second. 'I'm getting fed up with things being pinched from the mart.

Two things disappeared before the last sale, and now this. I think it's high time we called in the police.' He raised and lowered his chin a few times - another sign of his increasing agitation. He strode into his office and picked up his trilby from the hook behind the door.

The police station was situated not more than a hundred yards from the office in Norman Street. It was almost too handy, for our office was the first port of call should the police be looking for volunteers to participate in an identification parade.

Pulling on his trilby, Len strode towards the side door at the foot of the stairs, but before he reached it, he almost bumped into Sid Wheeldon, who had just made his way downstairs from the toilet.

'What's that you've got there Sidney?' asked Len, peering over the top of his spectacles at an object in Sid's hand.

'It's supposed to be an electric razor, but I can't get the damn thing to work,' growled Sid, 'I expect that's why it's in the sale.' He was totally oblivious to all the consternation he had just caused.

CHAPTER SIX

Miss Norman's sale & Ministry sales

Books at work, books at home,
Auctioneer on the roam.
Selling here and selling there,
First a cade lamb then a hare.
Turkeys, rose trees, loads of hay,
Everything goes on market day !

It takes some months for a novice auctioneer to settle down, and be able to pace himself to sell for hours at a time. I was no exception. A new auctioneer had really "arrived" when he was given a regular selling position in one of the main auctions within the cattle market.

Until that moment arrived, a new auctioneer usually held a roving commission. I sold fencing timber and sundries in the paddock at the rear of the market, loads of hay, straw and other produce, cade lambs in the spring, poultry and game, and turkeys at Christmas time. I also sold at the special sales of rose trees and shrubs, which we held occasionally. After the first few months, I was selling all the morning lots at the monthly furniture sales, and Alan sold the afternoon lots.

It was about this time that we held a special sale of furniture and antiques for Miss Elizabeth Norman of Asfordby Road, who was the daughter of the late E.R. Norman, Estate Agent, and kinsman of the Late Duke of Rutland. Miss Norman also had connections with the late John Ferneley, Melton's noted artist, who specialised in animal painting, especially horses.

The whole of the contents of the house were removed to the mart, where the cataloguing was carried out by Sid Wheeldon. There was a wonderful display of eighteenth and nineteenth century furniture, porcelain, glassware and silverware. It was the finest sale anyone could remember, and the firm has never had one quite like it since.

During the cataloguing of the sale, it was decided to call in an expert from Sothebys to examine the paintings and the drawings, with a view to including any of real value in a future Sotheby's sale. We were all surprised when the expert arrived. We were not expecting a young lady, and I was one of the sceptics who were murmuring that she didn't look old enough to have acquired that much knowledge. We were soon silenced, however, when she quickly identified a portfolio of sketches as being from the collection of Sir Joshua Reynolds. Each sketch had a small stamp mark in one corner.

She earmarked a few paintings for sale at Sothebys. Although she only came to examine the paintings, she did cast an admiring eye over the rest of the saleroom, where the tables were bedecked with old Derby and Worcester services, Chinese bowls and dishes, interspersed with ivory chessmen and old wine glasses with air twist and knopped stems. The room glowed with the patina on Regency and Sheraton furniture. Silver teaware and cutlery gleamed beneath the glass covers of the showcases. The walls were adorned with gilt framed mirrors and samplers, whilst added appeal was provided by a display of flintlock pistols, native spears, Kukris, broadswords and cutlasses.

The sale was a huge success, with high prices realised, and, in particular, for a painting "Vase with flowers," attributed to Rachel Raith. The painting had been overlooked by the young lady from Sothebys. The painting allegedly changed hands for a large sum over drinks at the nearby "Kings Head" after the sale.

All the general household wares were sold in the morning and not individually catalogued. Also in the morning sale, and not deemed worthy of a mention in the catalogue by Sid Wheeldon, were several trunks and boxes containing many books, which Sid had looked through and considered of little value.

I had taken an interest in old books, and decided to try and buy some of those in the sale. Much to my wife's dismay, I arrived home with three of the lots, and was immediately banished to the spare, empty bedroom with my books. I had spent fifteen pounds in total when my weekly income was only eighteen pounds, so my priority was to try and sell some of the books. I had already made some useful contacts through selling books, bought previously in the mart, to advertisers in the 'Exchange and Mart'.

When Sid discovered that I had paid fifteen pounds for the books, he told me that I was a bloody fool to pay so much for a load of rubbish. This remark rankled, and I was determined to prove him wrong. After poring over and sorting the books, I selected a few titles and wrote to one of my contacts, Mr Whiteson, in London.

Within three days I received a telegram, "Will arrive train Sunday p.m. to see books." At that time I had no car, so I couldn't pick him up from the station, but he duly arrived at my house, having walked well over a mile. He spent some time inspecting the books and selected about fifteen titles. Three of these he decided to take with him on the return journey, and I was to parcel up the remainder and forward by post. We agreed a price and he left a cheque for forty eight pounds. I know he received good value, for he left my house clutching a first edition by Dickens and two, vellum bound, editions by Oscar Wilde. For my part, I was over the moon with a return of over two hundred per cent on my initial investment, and even sweeter - I had proved Sid Wheeldon wrong.

Over the following few months I sold most of the remainder. Although, today, I regret the loss of the books, and would dearly love to have them on my bookshelves, at that time, with a young family, the money was more important.

When the euphoria over Miss Norman's sale had subsided, and the sweeping up had been completed, I noticed a broken picture frame protruding from one of the dustbins in the back yard. It had obviously been discarded as rubbish by Sid Wheeldon during the cataloguing of the sale. I removed it from the dustbin. Under the broken glass was an old sepia photograph of an elderly gentleman, seated on a dining chair with a top hat on the floor beside him. I was about to throw it back into the dustbin, when I noticed a faded piece of paper, with some handwriting on it, glued to the board beneath the photograph. Upon closer inspection, it appeared to be the bottom portion of a letter, and read, "your loving father J. Ferneley".

Possibly the only photograph of one of Melton's most famous sons, had been consigned to the dustbin, and almost lost forever. I rescued the photograph and took it home. Some years ago, at the request of Gilbert King, teacher and local historian, it was loaned to the Carnegie Museum in Melton, where it is still on display. A photographed copy hangs in the headmaster's study at the Ferneley High School in Melton, and I, too, have a copy.

The most lucrative sales for the firm during the fifties and early sixties were the Ministry sales, so called because they were held by order of the Secretary of State for Defence. They were held about three times a year, and comprised surplus machine tools, trailer vans, and stores and equipment of all kinds. The bulk of the items for sale were situated at the Ordnance Depot, Old Dalby, a village about eight miles from Melton, and were sold by catalogue in the mart or Auction Assembly Rooms, as the mart was so grandly titled in the catalogue.

Again, it was Sid Wheeldon who catalogued the sales, with Alan Brown as his assistant. It was no easy task, and Alan would regularly arrive back at the office, covered in grime and grease, the result of crawling under machines, looking for model numbers and other information. He was almost exhausted from manhandling electric motors and boxes of stores. Eventually, when Sid was in failing health, Alan took over the cataloguing of these sales.

My contribution to the preparation of these sales was being the firm's representative at the depot on viewing days. To reach the depot I caught the local train for Nottingham, which stopped at Old Dalby, and I returned, similarly, in late afternoon. My duties were to take prior

cash deposits for the sale, sell catalogues at one shilling each, and answer any queries about sale procedure. I took very few deposits as most intending purchasers had already made adequate banking arrangements. Representing the firm on these view days was probably the easiest task I had during my working life.

For most of the day, I sat in the site foreman's wooden hut, close to the entrance to the site, in the company of Margaret and Christine, two depot employees. I never did discover the exact nature of their jobs, but Christine was rather fond of fooling around. One day she "accidentally" tipped a bottle of perfume over my hair, drenching my clothes in the process.

When I boarded the train home that evening, I was acutely aware of the heavy fragrance which hung about my person, and which would drift into every corner of the carriage on the return journey. I glanced round the carriage and could hardly believe my luck when I spotted a heavily made up lady sitting close to the door. The carriage was only half full, so I was able to take a seat close to this lady. My fervent hope was that the overpowering fragrance would be attributed to her.

When we alighted in Melton, I walked a couple of paces behind her all the way into town until she turned right, and I turned left, but, by then I was almost home and dry. The only problem remaining was facing my wife. Would she believe such an unlikely story? Luckily, she did.

George Clarkson, from the Tanyard on Saxby Road, would, I'm told, often turn up at the office carrying a suitcase. He was not going on holiday, although our firm, in the past, had been agents for a cruise line. ('We did very little business, but I did get some cheap cruises,' said Arthur Shouler to me on one occasion.) George had called to pay for some livestock he had recently purchased. He opened the suitcase on the office counter and revealed the contents. It was crammed full with pound notes.

It was surprising how many people paid for their purchases at the Ministry sales in ready cash. Huge wads of notes were often pulled out of deep pockets for the cashiers to count. Periodically, through the sale day, I would discreetly leave the office for the bank with thousands of pounds stuffed in my raincoat pockets.

Those people who paid by cash, or had made prior financial arrangements with us, could take their release notes immediately and collect their purchases from the depot. Others had to wait until their cheques had cleared.

At one sale, one inoffensive looking little man paid by cheque for one small lot he had bought. The lot comprised a few boxes of miscellaneous items, and had cost only seven pounds. He asked if he could take his release note. At first Len Hewes refused, as the man had made no financial arrangements, but then relented and gave the man his release note. Len tried to justify his action by saying, after the man had left, 'Well, it was only seven pounds. If he hasn't got seven pounds he should never be in business.'

A few days later the cheque bounced. That was the only time I can remember anyone beating the release note system. Len was not at all pleased.

There was no lunch break during the Ministry sales. Arthur Shouler was the auctioneer, whilst his brother, Malcolm (Mac), booked out the sale. The third person on the rostrum was Mr Naylor, the man from the Ministry, who was there to look after the Ministry's interests in the items for sale. For the duration of the sale, Arthur's only sustenance was the odd sip of sherry. After the sale, the bottle was re-corked and carefully stored away in his office cabinet to await the next Ministry sale. It was rumoured in the office that he had the bottle marked.

The leisure time activities of the staff were varied. Jack was the secretary of the Hudson and Storer's charity. Alan played cricket for Egerton Park, a good local side. Curly stood as a bookmaker with Ernest Brown, a farmer from Old Dalby, at several racecourses, including, eventually, the Royal Ascot meeting. Stabby, apart from being a fervent Nottingham Forest supporter, also ran the football team in his home village of Stathern.

For several months, Stabby had been trying to persuade me to sign on for his club, Stathern Olympic, who played in the Melton League. He had obviously heard exaggerated accounts of my prowess on the football field. Eventually I relented and signed the form, which, surprisingly, he just happened to have in his top pocket. He also recruited a cattle market colleague, Alan Rowe, from Melton Farmers Ltd.

The village of Stathern nestled in the Vale of Belvoir, and the football pitch lay close to Belvoir Woods, which swept down the side of an escarpment. It was a typical village pitch with hassocks, cowpats and other rural hazards. A handful of supporters gave vociferous support, and any decisions made by the referee, which were not in favour of the home side, met with the usual vocal threat of a ducking in a nearby pond.

Stabby ran the club single handed. He was the manager, fixtures secretary, treasurer, trainer and groundsman. As there was no pavilion, all of the local players turned up already changed into football kit and ready to play. Alan Rowe and I received VIP treatment. Stabby and his wife, Edie, threw open their cottage door. We changed for the matches in their bedroom, and after every game we were given tea. Their hospitality was second to none.

CHAPTER SEVEN

On the move at work and home

From selling sheep to booking stores,
Another one of many doors.
New covered market comes at last,
Painting cattle now has passed.
Offspring numbers rise to three,
Plus a small blue car for me.

After eight years working alongside Sid Wheeldon in the sheep auction, I was at last given the opportunity to sell all the cull ewes on a regular basis. I had "arrived", but, unfortunately, not for long. Within a year, I developed ear problems, and had great difficulty hearing the spoken bids, especially those behind me. Reluctantly I had to give up selling and revert to booking.

It was shortly after I gave up selling that I moved departments for a third and final time. This time it was to the store cattle auction, after Stabby, who was the store cattle clerk, had left the firm.

There were only a few pens in the store cattle department, but there were two large bays, each of which could hold well over a hundred and fifty cattle. There was a salering, a weighbridge, and a wooden selling box on four iron wheels. Like the sheep pens, the cattle pens were open to the elements. For identification purposes, the cattle were marked with a dab of paint. All the beast to be sold in one bunch would be marked with a dab of red paint on the shoulder, the next bunch with a dab in the middle of the back, and so on until all possible marks had been used. The whole procedure would then be repeated with blue paint, then green, and so on. For each colour there were probably forty or fifty variations of marking positions. On a dry day the marks could easily be identified and the cattle drawn out of the hundred or so in the large bays, but if it was a wet day, the paint began to run. With the beast milling together, paint was often transferred from one beast to another, causing many problems.

Sandy Williamson, middle aged and rather portly, sported a bristly ginger moustache. He had been the foreman of the drovers for many years. It was Sandy who had a copy of the sheets and supervised the drawing out of the cattle at sale time. He had gained a certain reputation among the drovers, for it was rumoured that he had attained the same level of affluence as the auctioneer, simply by the amount of tips he received each week. Whilst this may have been a slight exaggeration, it was true that, with so many cattle in one bay, and some farmers eager to gain a more favourable slot in the order of sale, a few half crowns and the odd ten shilling note may well have changed hands.

When the new covered market was opened in 1968, and the store cattle housed in small pens, the writing was on the wall for Sandy. With the cattle now ticketed instead of being marked with paint, and a ballot for the starting pen, Sandy's influence was diminished. Whether Sandy's decision, to retire from the scene shortly after, was hastened by these events, we shall never know.

Our next door neighbours on Arden Drive were Mike and Eileen Button. Mike was the manager of a music shop, "White and Sentance", in Melton. They had two children, Anthony and Susan, who were about the same ages as our two children, Neil and Elaine. It was not long before Mike and Eileen produced another son whom they called Adrian.

Adrian grew into a mischievous, fair haired two year old, and was the delight, not only of the other Button children, but also of our two children.

'Why can't we have a baby brother like Adrian?' they would often chorus. We were not planning to have any more children, but, uncannily, shortly afterwards, we had another son, Paul. He grew into a mischievous, fair haired two year old, but now the chorus was entirely different.

'Mum, it's not fair. Paul keeps getting all our things out of the cupboard.' or

'Look what Paul's done. He's broken the wing off my plane.' In this case, the grass certainly looked greener on the other side.

The romance of the steam age enthralled many boys, including me. I was an avid trainspotter during my early schooldays. My two brothers carried on this fascination into their working lives. Both became footplate men on steam locomotives. Ray, who was two years my senior, had worked for many years on the footplate and had graduated from fireman to driver, regularly taking control of passenger trains. Although they both had steam running through their veins, both were to leave the railway within a short period of time. Ray took a job with Greengate and Irwell Ltd, a local rubber thread company, where the wages were much higher than on the railway. Railwaymen were not highly paid at that time. He told me later that he would still be driving locomotives if the pay would support his growing family, and I firmly believe he would.

Jeff, who is six years my junior, left and became a soldier with the Royal Anglian Regiment. He was posted to Watchet, on the Bristol Channel. He also owned a car. It was one of the first Minis produced, with the starting button located on the floor. When he was eventually posted abroad, he offered me the use of the car if I would fetch it.

'I have left it in the pub car park at Williton, a nearby village, and the keys are with the landlord,' he wrote. I had passed my test a few months earlier, but, with my growing family, I could not afford to buy a car.

Margaret and I decided to fetch the car one Saturday We left the children in the care of my mother in law, and caught the train for Birmingham. Here, we transferred to the "Cornishman", travelled down to Taunton, and caught a stop-go train to Williton.

We arrived at the pub at just about closing time after lunch, but just in time to snatch a quick half of scrumpy. When we emerged into the pub car park, it was almost empty, but there, in the far corner, stood a dejected looking blue Mini. When we inspected the car, we found there was no petrol in the tank, the battery and all the tyres were flat, and the handbrake was totally useless. Luckily, the pub was equipped with a petrol pump and airline, so two hurdles were soon overcome. We managed to start the car by pushing it round the car park, and, from that moment, I dare not stop the engine until we arrived safely back in Melton, several hours later. I now had a car, and I loved it.

In the store cattle auction, where previously we had one man with a paint stick, we now had two men, one with a glue stick, and one to stick on the lot tickets. Some of the drovers in the market were shift workers, locally employed and earning a little extra in their spare time, but most were farmers' sons and smallholders supplementing their incomes.

Some stayed only a short time, whilst others remained for years. Lou Sissons ticketed the store cattle for about ten years. Like Sandy Williamson, Lou had ginger hair, but sported long sideburns instead of a moustache. Lou was a man of instant decisions, but they were not always the right ones.

Six bales of bedding straw were left each Tuesday in the empty drawing pen. These were for strawing down the salering and the alley leading to the weighbridge. This task was normally carried out just before the start of the auction. On two consecutive Tuesdays, one of the bales had mysteriously disappeared whilst we were busy ticketing the cattle.

'Somebody's pinched a bale of straw again, Lou,' said Lenny Thornton, the glue man, 'That's the second time this month.'

'Right!' said Lou, emphatically, 'I'll catch the blighter next week.'

The following Tuesday, as we moved from pen to pen, ticketing the beast, Lou was trying to keep one eye on the drawing pen containing the bales of straw. This was not easy as there was so much concentration required whilst moving amongst cattle in a pen. As I stood outside the pen, with one foot on the rail, and book supported by my knee, I was almost bowled over as Lou suddenly rushed from the pen.

'There he goes,' shouted Lou, 'Hey! You! - stop. Where do you think you're going with that bloody straw?'

Lenny and I looked up the alley towards the weighbridge as Lou rushed towards a man carrying a bale of straw on his shoulder. Lou was still shouting at the man. 'Hey, where are you going with our straw?'

The man stopped and turned slowly round to face Lou. 'If you're talking to me young man,' he said quietly, 'I'll have you know I've just fetched this bale from my van to straw down my beast, and if you look, you'll find some more in there.' With that he turned away and continued his task, leaving a red faced Lou to mumble his apologies and return to his ticketing. The thefts never occurred again and the identity of the real thief was never discovered.

One of Lou's theories and one with which all drovers and clerks would probably agree, was that the nearer you stood to a beast, the less likely you were to receive a painful kick. If a beast's leg is at full stretch when it makes contact, the result can be excruciating pain, and I have seen drovers kicked with such force that they have been knocked out of the pen and across the alley. Keeping close to a beast tends to smother any kick before it gains momentum, but is not entirely hazard free, as Lou found out to his cost.

Lou leaned heavily against the rear of a big Friesian bullock, so that he could reach the adjacent beast to ticket it.

'Hey! Lenny, there's no glue on this one,' he shouted. But, before Lenny could get back into the pen to glue the beast, there was a sudden outburst from Lou.

'You dirty, filthy sod' he yelled at the beast he had been leaning on. He hobbled out of the pen, his wellington overflowing with brown puree. When cattle come to market straight off the grass, their motions are particularly loose, and Lou's wellington had been right in the line of fire. The other drovers rolled about the alley with glee as Lou retired, rather ruefully, to dry out his wellington with clean straw. I have always worn a pair of waterproof leg slips outside my wellingtons, which prevents an accident like this, but many drovers have never worn them.

Lenny grinned as he looked at Lou's cow muck spattered trousers, 'Ne'er mind Lou, it'll wesh out,' he said.

Working among cattle within the confines of the store beast pens carries obvious occupational hazards. I have seen drovers knocked over by beast and getting badly bruised in the process, whilst others have been kicked and despatched several yards away by the force of the blow. Often the resulting bruising and stiffness lasts for weeks. One of the most frightening experiences is to be "rolled" by a bunch of cattle. This happened to me on one occasion whilst standing in the alley between two rows of pens. Often the beast in a pen are brought out into the alley so that it is easier to glue and ticket them. I was trapped against the rail by a sudden surge by a bunch. As the bunch moved slowly along the alley, I was tightly "rolled" along the pen rails unable to do anything about the situation. Luckily for me, the drovers soon thinned out the bunch and I was able to extricate myself, suffering nothing worse than shock and a sore chest. It could have been much worse.

Some cattle have even tried to escape from the sale ring by rearing up and trying to clamber over the rails, a ploy which rarely succeeded, and if they did they were soon rounded up. One Tuesday, in the selling box, I was totally engrossed with my booking book when suddenly, a rather large Friesian heifer, which we were selling, reared up and planted its front feet firmly on my booking book on the lectern. Martin and I were suddenly confronted by the face of the heifer only inches away. There was not enough room in the box to accommodate all three of us, so, with plenty of verbal encouragement and slapping of hands, the heifer decided it was no longer a viable escape route and decided to withdraw. The only damage was to the booking book where the hoof and cow muck had ruined several pages. Again, it could have been much worse.

CHAPTER EIGHT

Cattle market bidding

The slightest twitch of thumb or lid
Are just but two of ways to bid,
But Martin sees his luck prevail
When a dog is bidding with its tail!
The auction will increase in pace
When a buyer comes from outer space!

Arthur Shouler's hair was not grey, it was almost white. It had changed colour almost overnight when he was a young man, and he was now over fifty. Arthur was an excellent auctioneer. He had the knack of keeping the store cattle auction alive with his wisecracks about the government and their agricultural policies. If "Rusty" Barnett, a rather deaf farmer who wore a large hearing aid with the control box on his chest, was present, Arthur's opening words were 'Are you tuned in Rusty?' This would raise a few smiles. Clever little phrases were also included in his general patter. These were aimed at extracting another bid when, moments before, the bidder had decided he had gone high enough.

'Best man will win,' he would shout laughingly, as two bidders were locked in earnest combat. Naturally, neither really wanted to appear second best.

'He's better looking than his father,' "buttering up" a farmer's son who was bidding at the auction for the first time, and had just been recognised by Arthur.

'Buy today - everybody will have their corn money next week and then they'll be dearer,' implanting this possibility into the minds of the cost conscious farmers. Like Sid Wheeldon, Arthur was always in the market early, penning and booking in stock, and was respected throughout the farming community. Whatever incident occurred during the auction, Arthur was always in control of the situation.

With the new covered market now in full swing, the next improvement to the facilities was the installation of a public address system. As the market was leased from the local council, after an initial period in the auctioneers' office, all announcements were made from the market superintendent's office. Loudspeakers were duly positioned in all the main buildings throughout the market. Whilst this new system was a boon to sightseers who had lost their children, or left their car lights switched on, or to farmers wanted on the telephone, it was a drawback to the auctioneer trying to conduct a sale with the p.a. loudspeakers set up in opposition. By this time we had a microphone and a couple of speakers at the ringside, but the comparison between the volume of the two systems was like comparing the squeak of a mouse to the roar of a lion, with our system being the mouse of course. To make matters worse, an inexperienced lady, reading out the messages, tended to shout into the microphone and repeat the messages three or four times. Arthur was not pleased.

'Now then gentlemen, four good Hereford steers, how much....'

'Would the owner of a blue Rover car, registration number....'

Arthur waited patiently until the message had been repeated four times and then resumed selling.

'From John Todd, gentlemen, there he is, stands behind them. Start me at three seventy, fifty then. At three forty only bid, at three forty two, four, six.....'

'Telephone call for Tony Bowley, telephone call for Tony Bowley, telephone call for Tony Bowley, in the superintendent's office.'

The voice blasting from the p.a. speaker completely drowned Arthur's attempts to conduct the sale. He bore these new intrusions with fortitude and patience for half an hour, but then he could stand it no longer. He slammed down his knocking down paper in disgust. 'Excuse me for two minutes, gentlemen,' he said before storming out of the selling box. Upon his return, he addressed his audience, 'Right, gentlemen, I've just given that woman a piece of my mind, and told her not to shout into the microphone and to announce messages no more than twice. Perhaps, now, we can get on with the sale.'

Arthur's outburst seemed to have done the trick. For a few weeks the messages were quieter and repeated less frequently. Things were not quite as frantic as they had been, but then, one Tuesday, the p.a. system boomed out again.

'Telephone call Hibbin's transport, telephone call Hibbin's transport, telephone call Hibbin's transport, telephone call Hibbin's transport.

Arthur looked across at me in despair. There was a new woman in the superintendent's office.

In addition to the special sheep sales, there were also special store cattle sales held in the autumn. With the advent of the covered market these sales were no longer held, but during the era of the open market they flourished, and attracted large numbers of cattle. The salerings were not used for these sales. Instead the selling box, which was mounted on four iron wheels, was dragged out onto the road between the sheep pens and the cattle pens. A circular area was strawed down for a salering, and all the buyers stood three or four deep around the perimeter to keep each lot in as they were sold. As each bunch of cattle was brought forward, this human sale ring opened up to allow the beast in. Similarly, they were allowed out, after the sale, on the opposite side of the ring. Many of these bunches were herded by drovers to the nearby L.N.E.R. railway station, and held in pens there ready for transporting later that day.

The selling box could comfortably hold two people, the auctioneer and his booking clerk, but, on many occasions, four or five people were crammed into the box. These extra people would include the owner of the lot being sold, possibly the owner of the next lot, waiting for his beast to enter the ring, and maybe a buyer trying to get a vantage point, or a dealer wanting to bid secretly. Sometimes it was difficult to move an elbow to write. I am reminded of this situation whenever I see an episode of 'Dad's Army', in which Captain Mainwaring's peaked cap and spectacles are knocked awry by the jostling of his squad in some confined space.

Like Sid Wheeldon, Arthur, too, had a little difficulty with names. Among the buyers there were always a few faces he knew well, but whose names he could not remember. One name in particular always caused some amusement because it only contained three letters - Key of Hungarton. To save him further embarrassment I wrote these names on the inside of the selling box, so that one glance was enough to jog his memory.

In later years, in the new market, the name of one buyer caused Arthur more trouble than any other. His name was Norman Hindson. On different occasions, Arthur called him Norman Hinchcliffe, Norman Hinchelcombe, and Norman Hinchley.

Luckily there was no need to write this name on the box as I knew it well

The most prevalent misconception about auction sales, and the reason that many people are deterred from attending one, is the belief that, should they inadvertently scratch their noses, or wave to friends, they might end up with an unwanted grand piano or even a pen of bullocks.

Nothing could be further from the truth. At worst, the auctioneer might use the incident to introduce a touch of humour to the proceedings.

'Madam, if you continue to wave to your friend, you will end up with a grand piano,' is usually sufficient to raise a few smiles. Any auctioneer, worth his salt, would recognise an intended bid as opposed to an unintentional gesture. If there is any doubt, a quick 'Are you bidding sir?' usually solves the problem.

'I can never see who's bidding,' said a friend to me one day, whilst discussing the store cattle auction. I was not surprised, as some buyers go to great lengths to disguise their bids.

People bid in many weird and wonderful ways. The flamboyant bidder will wave his arms and generally shout. During a livestock auction, a dealer will sometimes shout his bid to let other dealers know that he is "in", and not to take him out. Forming a ring, in which persons agree not to bid against each other, at any auction is illegal, but it is a practice which is extremely hard to prove. Other bidders are more secretive. A slight upward tilt of the chin, a twitch of the eye or corner of the mouth, a gentle lifting of a finger off the rail of the salering, are all the auctioneer requires to keep the price rising. An auctioneer soon familiarises himself with the methods of bidding used by his regular buyers, and is constantly aware of when they might bid, because he knows the preferences of those buyers. The less popular bidders, from an auctioneer's viewpoint, are those people who bid from behind with a hefty dig in the ribs, or a smart rap on the legs with a stick. It can be painful at times. Occasionally there are other methods.

The pre-arranged bid does not occur very often, and does not always have a satisfactory outcome.

'Here, Ken, have a toffee,' said Jack Wade, a cattle dealer and farmer. He always proffered a toffee before asking a favour. At other times he would be cadging a cigarette. 'It's only borrowed, It's only borrowed,' he would say, repeating every sentence as if to give added emphasis to his utterings. In all the years I knew him, not one cigarette was ever offered in return. Jack was a bustling impatient man, rushing around as though there was no tomorrow.

'I'm interested in that pen of horned Hereford bullocks at the bottom of the first alley,' he said, 'Do you know where I mean? Do you know where I mean?'

'Yes, I know the pen, Jack,' I replied, 'From Fairbrother of Gaddesby.' I looked at him, wondering what he had in mind, for he rarely told anyone which beast he was interested in.

'When those beast come into the ring, I'll be standing across the ring. When I want to bid I'll rest my stick on my shoulder like this,' he said, demonstrating his intentions, 'When I take it off, I've finished bidding. Have you got me? Have you got me?'

'All right, Jack, leave it to me. I'll prod Arthur while your stick's on your shoulder.'

'Good man. Good man,' said Jack, before bustling away. I made a note in the booking book to remind me of his elaborate plan to remain incognito whilst bidding for this pen of bullocks.

When the twelve bullocks eventually arrived in the ring for sale, they occupied a large proportion of the ring. This did not deter the few dealers who habitually stood in the ring, and I spotted Jack as he joined them across the ring.

As the bidding got under way, the other dealers were looking in Jack's direction, for they knew these were the type of bullocks he would normally buy. Jack stood impassively as he lit another "borrowed" cigarette, and casually rested his stick on his shoulder. I carried out my instructions, and nudged Arthur on Jack's behalf. The plan appeared to be working well, but suddenly, the beast surged across the ring towards the dealers, and Jack's desire to buy the beast took second place to the instinct of self- preservation. Down came his stick to ward off the milling cattle, and, in the ensuing melee, the lot was knocked down to somebody else. The best laid plans of mice and men.....

The rearing calf auction (often called the baby calves) had been in progress for some time before Alan Brown, the auctioneer, spotted the offender. When he first saw the small, elderly, man's action he thought he was mistaken, but when it occurred a second and then a third time, there was no mistake. The old man was definitely sticking out his tongue at Alan.

What does an auctioneer do in a situation like this? Should he jump down and punch the man on the nose? The man was frail and elderly, but, even if he had been young and strong, an auctioneer cannot allow himself to be drawn into any kind of brawl. Alan took what he considered to be the best course of action, and ignored the man and his rude gestures.

As the sale progressed, the man showed no other sign of emotion, but persisted in sticking out his tongue at Alan. The dealers were finding the situation amusing.

'I don't think he likes you, Alan,' shouted one.

'That's what he thinks of your selling,' shouted another.

Eventually the penny dropped with Alan - the old man was bidding. It was Alan's first encounter with old Mr Hubbard of Brentingby, but not the last. He was stone deaf, so how he knew the level of the bidding remains a mystery, for it must be difficult to lip read when an auctioneer is in full flow. This must be one of the most bizarre methods of bidding ever seen at an auction sale.

Eventually, Arthur handed over the reins of the store cattle auction to his son, Martin, who eventually became the senior partner in Shouler & Son. Arthur still sold for the first hour or so, but strange events were still taking place on a regular basis.

Bill Ross-Wilson, a former army tank commander and local councillor, farmed at Barsby, a village not far from Melton. Bill, a most amiable and outward looking man, kept a milking herd of Channel Island cows. Whilst the quality of the milk from these cows guaranteed an enhanced milk cheque every month, the cows were not so good at producing good beef calves. No matter how good a bull was used on the cows, the resulting progeny always lacked the conformation of good beef calves, and when sold later as strong stores, invariably sold for less than other popular beef crosses. It was a typical case of swings and roundabouts.

'Here comes Mr Setaside,' shouted Don Poyser, one of the drovers, as he spotted Bill arriving with two of his Charolais cross heifers in his trailer. The drovers had given Bill this nickname because of his enthusiasm for the new agricultural scheme by that name. Bill was accompanied by his black Labrador, Jupiter. It was obvious that some of his master's ebullience had rubbed off on him, for he ran from one drover to another, wagging his tail furiously.

When the time arrived for Bill's two heifers to be sold, he took up his position behind us in the selling box. The door of the selling box was left open, and I noticed two dealers just outside, sticks at the ready to tap Martin's leg when the bidding got under way.

When the bidding started it was painfully slow, as the heifers were not the best of sorts. Bill had almost resigned himself to a poor sale, when the tempo of the sale suddenly increased. The bidding was just becoming fast and furious when Martin whipped round angrily.

'For goodness sake, take your time,' he shouted to those standing behind, 'I can't take all those bids at once.'

Bill looked blankly at the two dealers standing outside the box, and they, too, were equally bemused, for neither had bid for the heifers for some time. The mystery was solved after the two heifers had been sold for a much higher price than anticipated.

Jupiter's tail had once more been wagging furiously, and bidding unwittingly by thumping against Martin's leg.

'Thank you very much, Martin,' said Bill as he patted Jupiter's head.

'They sold well,' said Martin, 'But it's a damn good job he didn't have the last bid,' he added, ruefully, after realising what had occurred.

The store cattle auction had just started when I spotted him. At first glances he appeared to be either a motor cyclist or an astronaut. He couldn't have been either, I decided, because he wore neither a space suit nor a set of leathers. In any case, I could tell he was much too old to be either. It seemed rather strange to see a man wearing a helmet with a large visor whilst also sporting a conventional jacket. Andy Wilson, a livestock transporter from Mansfield, who stood nearby, soon put me right, 'That's Geoff Wood from Mansfield, Ken, he wears that contraption for protection because he is allergic to dust'. The straw which we spread on the floor of the sale ring was not always of the best quality. Sometimes, the straw was old and crumbly and, when it got to that stage, it produced clouds of dust as the beast trampled it underfoot. For many years, Geoff had been an important buyer of meated heifers in the store cattle auction but it was the first time he had worn the new headgear in Melton market. He soon became a familiar figure in his new headgear and it didn't seem to affect his ability to spot a good heifer.

It was difficult for Martin to reach the store cattle auction after his short break in the market office before the start of the auction. The auction was often delayed as farmer after farmer waylaid him en route. Some wanted to talk about ongoing business with the firm, or to arrange future appointments. Others wanted advice. Running this gauntlet every Tuesday was the price he paid for being the firm's agricultural expert.

CHAPTER NINE

Pranks, luck money & lairage

How we deal with loads of luck,
Fancy dress and beast that's stuck.
Market jokers, pranks galore,
Singing dealer, eating straw.
Injured driver in the dead of night,
Wailing sirens and flashing light.

Some farmers were noted for their eccentricity of dress. Bill Rowlands, who had lived in North America for many years, always wore a stetson on his visits to the cattle market. Arthur Clark was always impeccably attired in a pin striped suit and bowler hat. He was seldom seen without a fresh rose or carnation in his buttonhole. It was Sam Frier's handkerchief, however, that took most people's eye. It was a huge red and white polka dot affair, which sprouted from his top pocket like a spray of flowers. I had a feeling that it was Sam's favourite handkerchief.

It came as a surprise when Sam appeared in the ring, one Tuesday morning, without his usual adornment. He had either dropped it somewhere or something more sinister was afoot, and it had been secretly whisked away. The loss had obviously upset Sam, for he appeared quite agitated. Despite peering into every nook and cranny around the ring, the handkerchief was nowhere to be found. A guardsman, on parade without his busby, would not have seemed more out of place than Sam without his handkerchief.

We did not have long to wait before the mystery was solved. After a few lots had been sold, a bunch of huge Friesian bullocks rushed off the weighbridge into the ring, and tied in a neat bow round the tail of one bullock was the missing handkerchief.

'There you are, gentlemen,' chortled Arthur Shouler, 'This lot comes with a posh bow thrown in as an extra.'

Sam was not enjoying the practical joke as much as the audience. His complexion had changed from its normal healthy red to a darker shade of purple, as he cursed the unknown perpetrator of this dastardly deed. The phantom joker of the store cattle auction had struck again.

The identity of the phantom joker did not remain hidden for long. Everyone had narrowed down the identity of the culprit immediately to two people, Jim Storer, a cattle lorry driver, or Curtis Machin, a prosperous, middle aged farmer, who farmed a thousand acres at Rotherby. Both men took an impish delight in playing pranks on others. This time the culprit was Curtis.

Wearing wellingtons, whilst attending the store cattle auction, always invited trouble when Curtis or Jim was around. Most weeks, several farmers would fall victims to the pea trap, where a few hard pea seeds were slipped, surreptitiously, into the tops of their wellingtons as they stood around talking. Only when they attempted to walk, did they discover how difficult it could be, and it was a familiar sight to see farmers emptying the pea seeds from their wellingtons.

The salering often resembled a circus as farmers and dealers walked around, blissfully unaware that the brims of their trilbys were full of empty cigarette packets and sweet wrappers. A group of dealers, standing just inside the ring, would suddenly discover that the straw under their feet had mysteriously burst into flames, causing a frantic stamping of feet to extinguish the flames.

The appearance of a nervous heifer always caused a certain amount of panic among those people in the ring, and a scramble to get out, much to the amusement of the farmers who were outside the ring. Some dealers, in the ring, who were wearing open, belted raincoats would attempt to make a quick exit, only to discover that their belts were tied to the rails behind them. It was common to see two or three raincoats dangling from the rails, where they had been hastily abandoned by their owners only moments before. This may have been one of the more dangerous pranks of the phantom joker, but, during all the years I worked in the store cattle auction, no-one was ever injured as a result of these pranks.

Curtis Machin was full of mischief and never missed an opportunity to play a joke on someone. I met him one day as I walked along Nottingham Street, and we paused for a chat just outside Tyler's Yard. Obsolete for some years, a dilapidated petrol pump, at the edge of the pavement, made an ideal support for Curtis' elbow as we discussed the store cattle trade in the previous day's market.

As we were talking, Curtis suddenly nudged me with his elbow. 'We've got a customer, Ken,' he said, grinning.

I looked round to see that a sports car had just pulled up close to the old pump. Out of the car stepped a smartly dressed young lady.

'How many gallons my dear?' asked Curtis, gripping the nozzle of the pump.

'Oh! dear! I don't want any petrol - I was just parking - I didn't realise....' She broke off, confused and rather embarrassed, jumped back into the car, and drove off.

'Well damn me!' said Curtis, 'And I was only just starting on her.'

'You are a devil, Curtis, you'll be landing yourself in hot water one of these days with one of your pranks' I said.

Curtis grinned. 'You've got to have a bit of fun. It'd be a poor old world if we didn't have a laugh now and then. Do you know, you can tell some people anything and they'll believe you - providing you keep a straight face.'

'How do you mean?' I asked, sensing another tale.

'I happened to be talking to two farmers in the market tearoom last week, when one of them asked me how my son, John was keeping - you know he's recently had one of these new hip replacement operations, don't you?' I nodded. 'Well, I told them that he doesn't get any pain, but the joint does tend to squeak a bit, now and then. The surgeon was marvellous though, he fitted a small grease nipple to the side of the hip. Now John gives it a few shots with a grease gun when it squeaks, which soon puts matters right.'

'Gerrout ! Well I'll be blowed !' was all they could say, and their faces were an absolute picture.

'I wish I'd been there, Curtis,' I said. I could have listened to his tales for hours, but we had to part company, and I left him still leaning on the pump, probably awaiting his next "customer."

Later, the role of the store cattle prankster was taken over by a young dealer, Keith Arnold. The type of prank, though, changed little, like hiding the auctioneer's knocking down paper. Market auctioneers rarely use a gavel. Our paper was a rolled- up copy of the "Farmers Weekly". This makeshift gavel had been going strong for many years, and repaired with Sellotape on a weekly basis. Other pranks in his repertoire were switching off the amplifier whilst the auctioneer was in full flow, and jamming a stool under the knob of the door to the selling box to prevent our exit.

We are all creatures of habit, and the habits of farmers vary little from those of their animals. Just as the dairy cows amble into the same stalls each milking time, so the farmers and dealers take up the same positions around the salering each week.

Fred Siddans and George Hobill always sat close to the selling box to our left, whilst Bill Tabener and John Bergin sat to our right. During the auction, I could often hear Fred quietly humming a tune, but with John Bergin, a popular Irish cattle dealer, the musical interludes were much louder. In addition to his humorous quips, he would frequently burst into song, and treat everyone to a few lines of an Irish folk song.

John always brought with him a pack of sandwiches, which he proceeded to consume whilst the auction was in progress. Whenever he bought a lot, he would leave his sandwiches, including the one he was eating, on the lectern close to the auctioneer, whilst he nipped out to examine the beast he had just bought.

During one of these temporary absences, Keith Arnold slipped a piece of straw into John's half eaten beef sandwich, fully expecting John to spit out the first mouthful upon his return. To everyone's astonishment, John tucked into the remainder of his sandwich with relish, completely unaware of the added nutrient. There were a few chuckles all round but the prank had fallen short of Keith's expectations as there was no reaction from John.

Keith did not have things all his own way, however, and the tables were turned in a most unexpected way one Tuesday, when he became the object of, rather than the perpetrator of, the schadenfreude, so peculiar to many farmers,

Cows, with suckling calves, were always sold at the beginning of the auction, before the store cattle. It was wise to treat all cows, with calves at foot, with caution, especially as they were in a strange environment in the cattle market, and the protective maternal instinct was much in evidence.

Keith, who often bought cows and calves, was always accompanied by a working collie. The dog was lying just outside the salering, close to where Keith was standing inside the ring, with its nose just poking under the bottom rail. When a Friesian cow and her calf entered the ring, the cow spotted the dog and her protective instincts came to the fore. With head lowered, she charged across the ring towards Keith and his dog. The only escape route was up and over the rails of the salering, but there was one drawback. The rails were covered with smooth, slippery zinc sheets. With his arm over the top rail, Keith pulled himself up, but the cow was much quicker. He had scrambled only half way up when the cow butted him from underneath. Keith shot upwards, and, when gravity completed the cycle, the cow duly obliged again, and again, and again, until helping hands from grinning farmers dragged him over the top. It was fortuitous that the cow had no horns, or the consequences could have been more serious than the bruising he received to his backside. Here was the perpetrator of so many pranks on the receiving end for a change, but it didn't stop him for long.

Ken Armstrong was another farmer who did a bit of dealing. Ken, who farmed at Grace Dieu near Belton, Loughborough, would always arrive at the cattle market after calling at Beavers' cake shop in Scalford road. The paper bags he carried were full of assorted cream cakes and these were distributed amongst the clerks and drovers in the store cattle auction. He also owned a small cattle lorry and always kept a few boxes of biscuits in the cab. A box would be handed out as a reward for a special favour. Although possessing such a generous nature, Ken's language tended to be a little on the blue side. At the time when the Ministry of Agriculture was trying to encourage the rearing of polled cattle only, and markets were instructed to pen and sell horned cattle separately from polled cattle, Ken said to me one Tuesday whilst we watched a farmer unload two horned beast, 'If they were my beast I'd have had them f****** horns off with a pair of f****** bolt croppers.' Whether he actually performed such an operation, I never discovered, but horned cattle always made less at auction than polled cattle. Apart from the injury horns can inflict, more cattle per trough can feed in the yards during the winter if they are polled.

Ken was astute and could often see where a quick profit was to be made in the cattle market. One Tuesday he bought a young Friesian heifer in the Dairy auction. The vendor was a young farmer, who was more interested in seeing the heifer go to a "good home" than any commercial consideration. He and his wife were horrified to see the heifer appear for sale again in the store cattle ring. They were so afraid that the heifer would be bought to slaughter, which it probably would have been, that they bid for the heifer, bought it back at a higher price than the dairy auction price, and took it home again. The trading was perfectly legal. Ken made a quick profit but it was not a good day for the young couple who made a considerable loss

Another tradition in livestock markets is the practice of offering "luck money". This practice seems to puzzle many visitors to the market, and can be best explained as an inducement to bid. When a vendor offers a fiver or tenner for "luck" during the sale of his cattle, he is telling the assembled buyers that the person who eventually buys the beast will receive the money as a gift or reward.

Frank Gilman, a businessman and racehorse trainer from Morcott in Rutland, who trained Grittar to win the Grand National, bought many store cattle in Melton market each year. Frank, who was rather flamboyant in character, would appear suddenly in the auction, buy several lots of cattle in a short period of time, then disappear just as quickly. Frank would pocket the fivers and tenners which were offered as luck money, but would never be bothered with the one pound notes which were offered. He would stuff these into the top pockets of farmers standing next to him, and I have seen a few children in pushchairs leave the ring side with pound notes clutched in their tiny hands. He once tore a pound note into two pieces, giving one piece each to the two drovers in the ring.

It was Ken Botterill from Waltham, however, who held decided views about luck money. He maintained that, to gain the most advantage, there was a "precise moment" during the bidding to offer the luck money - not too early and not too late. One Tuesday, Ken put this theory to the test in the store cattle auction.

Ken had many contacts, and often looked after the interests of vendors who could not attend the auction. Ken did some dealing himself, so he did not want others to know of his connection with these beast.

'Take these three five pound notes,' he said to me, just before the start of the auction, 'Put a fiver on each of the three lots of beast, but offer it only when I give you the signal.'

'What will the signal be, Ken?' I asked.

'I'll stand near the gate with a cigarette in my mouth. Offer the luck money when I take the cigarette out of my mouth.'

'Right!' I said, slipping the fivers under the booking book. Ken would often keep a cigarette in his mouth for long periods, allowing the ash to form in a long curl on the end, and rarely taking it out of his mouth, so there was nothing unusual in this simple arrangement.

When the first lot of beast entered the ring, Ken had taken his place by the gate, and was just lighting a cigarette. The bidding was brisk, and, within a couple of minutes, the cigarette was out of his mouth, the luck money offered and the beast duly sold.

Everything was going according to plan, and the half smoked cigarette was back in his mouth as the next lot entered the ring. The bidding had only just started, when there was an interruption to the sale. A dealer had spotted a small lump on the neck of one of the beast.

A few more minutes elapsed whilst the beast was turned around and inspected.

'Right, gentlemen, I'll start again, and I declare one of the beast to have a small wen on its neck,' shouted Martin, the auctioneer.

I glanced across at Ken as the sale re-started. The cigarette was so small that it was almost burning his lips. He raised his chin and moved his head from side to side to avoid the fumes. Finally he could bear it no longer, and quickly nipped the butt out from between his lips. His plan had misfired, for I followed his instructions to the letter, and I am sure we were nowhere near his "precise moment" when we offered the luck money. However, Ken was not deterred, and there was a fresh cigarette in his mouth for the third lot.

It is customary for farmers, who are offering cattle for sale in the market, to interest as many potential buyers as possible in the cattle. Many farmers would stand outside the pen with a prospective buyer and discuss the attributes of their cattle, but that was not Jack Appleby's way.

Little Jack, who was about five feet four in his boots and gaiters, stood in the pen, cleaning down his six Friesian bullocks with a handful of straw. He was not in the least intimidated by the size of the beast as they towered above him.

'Gerrout you big sod,' he shouted, as one of the bullocks threatened to pin his diminutive frame against the rails. He dug an elbow into the side of the bullock, and it obliged by moving over. 'There y'are, George, just the right sorts for you,' he said to the farmer, who was watching from outside the pen. George Hobill rubbed his bristly moustache with the back of his hand, replaced his pipe in his mouth, and smiled benevolently at little Jack.

'I might be interested if you take out that little devil, and sell 'em five and a one,' said George, teasingly, trying hard to keep a straight face.

'Gerraway, George, they're like peas out of a pod. There ain't a pin to choose between 'em,' said Jack.

'Will there be plenty of luck money if I buy 'em?'

'Course there will, if they make a good price, you know that, George.'

'We'll wait and see then,' said George, and, as he walked away down the alleyway, he could hear little Jack already tackling another potential buyer.

'Hey Bill! These beast are just what you're looking for.'

There were over six hundred cattle to sell, and, as the hand bell was rung to summon buyers from around the market, little Jack took his place at the ringside to await the arrival of his beast in the ring. Jack preferred to shout the praises of his cattle from there rather than stand behind the auctioneer in the box.

The sale had been in progress for about half an hour, when I noticed Jack climb to the top rail of the ring. I glanced at the booking book. Jack's beast were not due to be sold for at least another half an hour. As the next lot, six big Friesian bullocks, rushed off the weighbridge, little Jack, from his precarious perch, was already in full voice.

'They're all right and straight, Mr Shouler. I'll stand behind 'em. They'll do anybody good, and there'll be a tenner for luck if the price is right.'

Arthur glanced at the booking book. 'Have we got the right vendor down?' he whispered.

'I'm positive,' I replied. 'His beast are due in about half an hour.'

Arthur turned towards little Jack. 'Now then, Jack,' he chortled, 'These are not your beast, you know.'

Little Jack bristled with indignation, and almost fell from his perch as he gesticulated with his arms. 'Of course they're my bloody beast,' he yelled, 'I should know my own beast. I've shepherded 'em all summer.'

'Hang on a minute, Jack,' said Arthur, 'Before you blow a fuse, just pop out and see if your beast are still in the pen you've stood in all morning.'

Reluctantly and disbelievingly, little Jack climbed down and wandered off, still muttering to himself. Like a few more farmers, he had not yet grasped the method of the new ballot system for the order of sale, and relied on recognising his beast as they entered the ring.

Half an hour later, as six more big Friesian bullocks entered the ring, Jack appeared again on the top rail, a tenner clutched in his raised hand. Quite oblivious to the good natured leg pulling around him, he shouted once more.

'These are my beast Mr Shouler. They'll do anybody good. I've shepherded 'em all summer.'

'There you are gentlemen,' laughed Arthur, 'These beast really are from Jack Appleby, who'll start me?'

Quite often, during the busy periods of spring and autumn, I would stay behind in the market to supervise the stock leaving the market, and deal with any overnight lairage. Sometimes the lairage would be pre-arranged, and could be dealt with early in the evening, but, occasionally stock would be left accidentally, or by some misunderstanding between the buyer and the transporter.

Harold Bradshaw, the foreman in charge of Harvey Brothers transport, would always keep me informed about the expected times of arrival of his lorries to collect store cattle and barren cows. 'Herbert will be here about half past ten tonight for the last load, Ken,' he said to me one Tuesday.

'O.K. Harold, I'll be around. The rear gates will be open.'

Five sets of gates were open during market day, but only the rear gates remained open for the late collection of stock. When all the overnight lairage had been attended to, and all other stock had been collected, I sat in my car to await the arrival of Herbert in his articulated lorry. I glanced at my watch - it was almost ten o'clock. If he was on time, it would take about fifteen minutes to load the cattle, another five minutes to lock up, and then five minutes to get home in the car. With a bit of luck I should be home by eleven o'clock, but it wasn't to be. Herbert arrived after eleven thirty. I was not too pleased.

'Where the devil have you been Herbert?' I asked sharply.

'Sorry, Ken, I had a breakdown'

'Never mind, let's get you loaded up and away.'

Herbert could see I was annoyed, so said no more. I had already switched off most of the lights in the cattle shed, leaving just one row on to enable us to load. The residents of houses close to the market had often complained of late night activity and noise from the market, so we tried to be as quiet as possible on such occasions.

Bang! The tailboard of Herbert's lorry hit the concrete loading bay. I winced as the noise resounded through the cattle shed like an exploding bomb. The two springs supporting the tailboard were badly sprained, and could not let the tailboard down gently as they should.

'It's about time your firm replaced those springs, Herbert,' I said, despairingly.

Herbert said nothing. We set about the task of loading the beast, and within twenty minutes they were all loaded. As the springs were sprained, it took both of us to lift up the heavy tailboard. I walked back into the pens, leaving Herbert to fasten the retaining bolts on the tailboard. I don't know exactly what happened next, but as I walked away, there was another loud crack as the heavy tailboard descended on Herbert's head. I whipped round, but all I could see was an arm sticking out from underneath.

I rushed forward, fearing the worst. I thought it had killed him. Somehow, I managed to lift the tailboard and drag him out. He was semi- conscious and moaning. Blood poured down over his face. I had no first aid skills, but I propped him in a sitting position against the rails, and made him as comfortable as I could with an old coat.

'Hang on, Herbert,' I said, 'I must get some help.' There was no response from Herbert - just a continual moaning. I felt helpless and desperate. I rushed to the nearby exit gates, hoping to get some help from a passer-by. There was no-one around. Then I remembered it was past midnight.

I jumped in my car and sped the short distance to the telephone box in Nottingham Street, and rang for an ambulance. I waited on Scalford Road to direct the ambulance into the rear of the market. Within a couple of minutes a police car arrived, then another police car, closely followed by an ambulance. They all followed my car into the market. As we neared the store cattle pens, my car headlights picked out the figure of a man. He was walking around, smoking a cigarette. It was Herbert. Thank God he's O.K., I thought, but then I went cold. I had just made an emergency call, fetched out two police cars and an ambulance to a man walking around, smoking a cigarette. I would probably be charged with wasting police time.

I need not have been concerned. I think the policemen and the ambulance men were relieved to see him on his feet after my pessimistic assertion that he was almost dead when I left him. The gaping wound to Herbert's head was quickly examined.

'Come on old chap, let's have you inside the ambulance for some treatment,' one ambulance man said. Herbert moved towards the ambulance, but then, to everyone's amusement, he sat down on the vehicle steps and carefully pulled off his wellingtons before clambering aboard. Soon there was a small pile of swabs accumulating on the floor of the ambulance, as they stemmed the flow of blood and dressed the wound. When they had finished and Herbert was re-united with his wellingtons, one of the policemen took Herbert gently by the arm

'How far have you got to travel with these cattle?' he enquired.

'I'm heading for Boston,' replied Herbert.

'Well, if you feel at all groggy, just pull off the road for a rest,' said the policeman.

As a final gesture, and to show that he still retained his faculties and his sense of humour, Herbert turned towards the policemen. 'Seeing as you blokes are here, I'd better fill in my movement book,' he said.

The policemen smiled, benevolently, and took their leave, following the ambulance out of the market. It had been an eventful evening, and, as I drove home in the early hours, I wondered what the nearby residents had made of the sirens and the flashing blue lights in the cattle market.

Apart from the cattle left overnight on a Tuesday, we also took in up to a hundred cattle for lairage on a Monday evening ready for the sale the next day. I also carried out this task. The pens in the dairy shed were used for this purpose. One dealer, Ernie Wardle from Bakewell, would often telephone me at home, early on the Monday morning to book pens for lairage that day.

'Just gorrup 'as thee? I shall 'ave about thirty today. I'll bring some 'ay with me tonight.'

The cattle had to have a plentiful supply of hay and water, and the pens were bedded down with straw. Although we encouraged farmers to bring their cattle for lairage during the late afternoon, there were always some who brought them during the evening, and I was often there until after nine o'clock.

One Monday, when the last load was safely penned, and the lorry had gone, I had only to fetch three more bales of hay from the fodder store, then I was finished for the day. I transported the bales on a hand trailer, which was kept in the store for this purpose. I left the three bales in the centre of the alley next to the pens of beast to be fed, but before removing the binder twine and distributing the hay to the beast, I decided to return the trailer to the store. This proved to be a mistake I was never to repeat.

I was away only five minutes, but when I returned I was horrified to find that the impatient cattle had been trying to reach the sweet smelling hay by thrusting their heads through the pen rails. One steer, with large horns, had somehow wriggled its head between the bottom two rails of the pen, in a vain attempt to reach the hay, and was now stuck fast, by the horns, in a kneeling position.

With no-one around to assist, I had to try and free the steer myself. I tried twisting its head by grasping its horns, I pushed and shoved, but to no avail. After transferring the rest of the cattle to another pen, I even tried pulling it round by the tail. A feeling of desperation and near panic was beginning to set in. What could I do? The steer was making gurgling noises, and its eyes rolled upwards in their sockets.

Although I felt helpless, I suddenly had an idea. I jumped in my car and raced the half mile home as fast as I could. I grabbed my hydraulic car jack from the garage, and within a few minutes I was back in the market. The steer had not moved an inch. I set up the jack between the two rails as close to the steer's head as I could get and pumped away with the handle. The rails were forced apart under the intense pressure, and, with a minimal amount of assistance from my foot, the beast extricated itself from its predicament. I leant against the rails for a few moments in sheer relief. I had learned a little more about the behaviour of cattle, and realised what a wonderful invention the hydraulic jack was. I was certainly thankful for it on this occasion.

The rails of the pen, which were made at the beginning of the twentieth century, were of solid iron construction, unlike the tubular steel ones in the modern cattle market. The two rails are still bent to this day, and, whenever I see them, I also see that steer with its eyes rolling upwards in their sockets.

CHAPTER TEN

Woolsheets & rent collecting

Sewing patches onto bags,
Working just like two old lags,
But the rent rounds prove to be
Such a boon with food and tea.
We conclude with just a little
Of obnoxious flying spittle !

By the time I joined the firm, the annual wool sales in the cattle market were no longer taking place. The only remaining relic of those sales was the large set of iron wool scales, which was now tucked away in the corner of the wool room above the mart. Farmers now sent their wool directly to the wool merchants. We supplied wool sheets for two merchants, Pearces of Thame, and Greenhoughs of Bradford. The sheets would arrive in huge bales, which were hauled up on the pulley to the wool room, prior to sorting.

During the winter months, the male clerks, usually Stabby and I during my early years, would spend any available spare time sorting out the woolsheets. The sheets were like huge hessian sacks, and each one was spread out on a large table, and its capacity assessed. Some would hold ten fleeces, others twenty and so on.

Any sheets with holes were repaired with patches, using a thick six inch long needle, rather like prisoners sewing mailbags. The sheets were then individually rolled up, tied with string, labelled, and stacked in piles against the walls. The farmers collected their woolsheets from us in the spring, just before clipping time. Sometimes we would send them by rail or bus. Some of the larger farms required a lot of sheets, and we would roll these into a large bale.

Assisting me in the wool room one day was Colin, the new office boy, and we had just prepared such a bale ready for collection by the railway lorry, but first we had to lower the bale from the wool room on the pulley.

'Now then Colin, I want you to go downstairs and take the strain on the rope. When I give the signal, I'll push the bale through the trapdoors,' I said.

Colin followed my instructions and took hold of the rope. What I had forgotten to tell him, however, was to wrap the rope a couple of times round the pillar in the mart so that the friction would retard the rate of descent. The bale turned out to be heavier than Colin, albeit not a lot, so that when I pushed the bale over the edge with my foot, the bale descended smoothly as Colin ascended still clinging manfully to the rope. Luckily he was not injured, and I had learned yet another lesson.

Between market days, the very nature of our business meant that there were surprises and touches of humour around every corner. Routine work had to be carried out, but even this could be eventful at times. Rent collecting provided an opportunity to get out and about in the town. Every Monday morning three clerks would set off on their rounds, usually after a quick cup of coffee at Freeborough's café in Sherrard Street. Each collector knew where the next cup of tea would be offered. On Stabby's round there would be cheese sandwiches in Brook Street, a cup of tea in Bishop Street, and a sip of sherry elsewhere.

On the country village round, the biggest problem was getting away from some of the tenants, who looked forward to the visits of the rent collector, the postman and other tradesmen. For some of the older tenants it was a chance to have a chat, and they made the most of it. My younger brother, Jeff, who became a postman after he left the army, told me that one or two elderly people in the villages relied on the goodwill of the postmen to collect their pensions and bring a newspaper for them - vital social functions which should never be overlooked.

Being estate agents, we had to deal with hundreds of tenants. With an agricultural business like ours, we not only had tenants of private flats and houses, but also tenants of farms, land, and even a batch of allotment gardens between the the play close and the railway station.

The most common complaint from tenants was that improvements and repairs are not being carried out as they should be. Some were justified, many were not. We wrote to one dear old lady to inform her that her landlord wished to install a new bathroom in her house. She replied to say that it would be very nice, but that she couldn't be doing with all the upevil (*sic*) at the moment.

Most allotment holders are keen gardeners, and it is understandable that, when one allotment is neglected in the midst of all the other well-tended allotments, acrimony will set in. As the seeds from weeds sweep over the other allotments, the complaints begin. This was the case when Rex Holder neglected his allotment and used it for storing all manner of things.

We had already received a few complaints from adjacent tenants, and had written to him several times, but had not reached the stage of serving him with a notice to quit. One of the tenants went to great lengths to take a leaf out of our book by compiling, typing, and sending to us an inventory of the items on Rex Holder's allotment. I believe this to be the most original method of complaining we ever received from a tenant. The inventory was neatly presented and contained a list of items comprising 2 x 50 gallon water butts, washing machine, corrugated sheet, 5 baths, bed headboard, guttering, barrel, sawing horse, door, wheelbarrow, wire fencing, metal crate, car tow bar, leaf spring, aprox. 1 ton assorted timber, broken lawnmower, 2 sweet jars, drying machine, 2 windows, 2 large paraffin cookers, 2 sinks, chimney top and cowl, milk churn, plough shear, 2 buckets, 6 plastic bags containing garden and household rubbish, 3 wire baskets, 1 large chicken hut filled with various rubbish, and many more items.

The tenant also stated that half the allotment was cultivated by a friend of Mr Holder, so all these items lay on one half of the allotment. Rabbits lived under the chicken hut. A prolific crop of weeds grew each year and their seeds were blown across all other allotments.

How could you not take notice of such an original complaint, especially when it is so neatly presented, with sheets typed and properly fastened together.

In the store cattle auction there were constant smiles at some of the notes sent in by farmers about their cattle. There were "Baron cows" and "Carves" entered often in the market, and when the relatively new continental breeds, such as the Charolais, Limousin, and Simmental started to appear in the British countryside, they caused pronunciation and spelling problems for many farmers, and for a few clerks too. One local farmer, delightfully, called his cattle "Sentimentals" - a much better name whichever way you look at it.

Cattle came from far and wide across the country to be sold in the store cattle auction. We even had cattle from Wales and Ireland. One farmer from Derbyshire sent in a note with his cattle written on the side of a shredded wheat packet. It read, very precisely, "Home bred and reared at 1034 ft above sea level on limestone at Tideswell, Nr. Buxton, Derbys. Poor pasture, short of grass, need worm drenching and some good Melton grass." What more could he say?

Almost without exception, the livestock lorry drivers were, and probably still are, the salt of the earth. In addition to doing a dirty job, they also faced the risk of being kicked every time they loaded a bunch of cattle. Despite this they seemed to love their occupation. They would help out with the penning of cattle in the market, and would look after the interest of their firm's farmer clients, who had just bought cattle, by putting the various lots together in the pens so that loading was easier later in the day. They also loved a bit of humour.

One Tuesday I was talking to Alan Hinch, who drove a livestock lorry for Hibbins' Transport.

'I've not seen anything of Terry Woods lately, Alan, is he OK?'

'You mean old "Gobber" - yeah, he's OK,' said Alan with a grin. 'I moved some beast for him yesterday and he rode with me in the lorry.'

Terry was an Irishman who lived at Frisby and dealt in cattle to a small extent. He loved a drink and also chewed tobacco. Chewing tobacco produces a copious amount of saliva and this has to be jettisoned at regular intervals. Terry was adept at discharging this missile of brown saliva through clenched teeth with unerring accuracy - hence the nickname "Gobber".

'Yes he was chewing the cud again while he sat next to me in the lorry yesterday,' Alan continued, 'I had my window down but it's a bit disconcerting while you are driving along to suddenly see this brown bullet of spittle hurtle past your face and out of the window.'

'You'll really have to get a spittoon fitted in your cab, Alan,' I said jokingly, 'The draught might just blow it back in through the window next time.'

CHAPTER ELEVEN

Dealers, escapes, Sam, & sheets

Dealer's merits, beast that flee,
Bantams living in a tree.
Heifer cracks shop window pane;
Then up some stairs and down again.
Sam gets wet on his big day out,
But it's not the rain that made him shout !

Over the years dealers have not enjoyed a good image. People always tend to be wary of items or livestock offered for sale by dealers. Whilst booking in store cattle, I was asked the same questions many times during the course of the morning. 'Whose beast are these? They're not dealer's beast are they?' I have never understood this aversion to dealers' cattle. If they are good beast, and they can't be bad if they have just caught the eye and prompted the question, it matters little who the owner is. They may belong to a dealer today, but yesterday they probably belonged to a farmer. A few lots of cattle are "hawked" from market to market, but generally dealers' cattle are turned over in a short period. Dealers usually put a reserve price on their cattle, but then, so can farmers if they wish. Many of the cattle offered for sale by dealers have been bought privately straight from farms. The biggest fear among some farmers seems to be that, if they buy dealers' cattle, they will pay an inflated price for them. However, the dealers have probably paid less than market value when buying the cattle, and this margin is where the profit lies.

There are exceptions to every rule, but most of the cattle dealers I have known in Melton market have been honest and straight men, who would stand behind their beast, and take back a beast should anything prove to be wrong with it. Dealers have to be astute to be successful. I have often seen a dealer buy a single beast in the ring, and place it in with a pen of similar cattle, which he had for sale later in the auction. The single beast matches the others so well, that, when that pen is sold, the dealer makes a good profit on the odd beast simply because bunches of cattle usually make more money per head than beast sold singly. This is just good business.

Dealers also study the buyers carefully. They know which breeds certain farmers buy, and when a farmer starts to buy his store cattle one week, the dealers will be selling some of his favoured breed the following week. If a farmer has been buying, the auction is almost over, and a dealer thinks the farmer needs some more cattle to make up his load, the dealer will offer, for a second time, at the end of the auction, suitable lots which were "bought in" the first time they were offered - a ploy which is quite often successful.

Two of the most likeable dealers were the Hall brothers, David and Ray, from Langley Mill. Brothers they were, but as different in appearance and character as chalk and cheese. Big David, as he was affectionately called, was tall and stocky, and had the most infectious laugh. Ray, however, was of a more wiry build and quieter in character.

Without hesitation, and without being asked, they would pitch in to help whenever we experienced difficulties in the running of the store cattle auction. Whenever we had a beast in trouble, they were there. One Tuesday a Friesian steer had slipped and turned onto its back in the numbering race (a narrow zinc sheeted alley), and lay there, feet in the air, unable to get back onto its feet. It was David who commandeered a rope from the dairy auction, and, with assistance, dragged the steer out backwards, so that it could stand up again. Ray would often help in the salering during the auction, and they would often glue and ticket their own cattle. Always ready with his quips, David spotted the drovers trying to move a Murray Grey heifer down the alley, 'Now then, lads,' he shouted, 'You know you can't hurry a Murray!' When giving instructions on how to number his cattle, he would say, 'Eight look-alikes together,' or 'They're all one bundle.'

One Tuesday, during the cattle auction, I felt a tug on my smock from behind. I glanced round, but could see no-one. Then I felt it again. I glanced round again - still no-one. 'Psssst, Psssst,' hissed somebody. I looked round then down, and there, crouched very low, was Ray, trying to hand me a card with reserve prices on it. He didn't want anybody in front of the selling box to see what he was doing.

One of the most astute dealers I have known was Tony Key from Norwich. Ably assisted by John Fox, Tony was always in the market early in the morning to draw and pen his cattle. He would often show over fifty cattle, but rarely needed any assistance from the drovers. He would hand me a card on which he had listed all his lots and pen numbers. This enabled us to ticket his cattle without any difficulty. His astuteness was confirmed by the reputation he held amongst his fellow dealers.

On the occasion of his daughter's wedding, Tony laid on a lavish reception, to which many of his fellow dealers were invited. The following week I met Bill Harvey, from Norwich, a fellow dealer, who had attended the wedding.

'How did the wedding go then, Bill?' I asked.

'Oh, fine,' Bill replied, 'All the drinks were free, so I had plenty.'

'Wasn't that taking advantage of his generosity a bit?' I queried.

Bill looked at me and smiled. 'Not a bit of it,' he said, 'I knew damn well he would have the cost back out of me within a couple of weeks, so I made the most of it.' - a testament, indeed, to Tony's business acumen, from a fellow dealer.

Wherever there is a public auction, there are dealers, whether they are livestock dealers in cattle markets, fine art dealers in the upmarket auction houses in London, or second hand furniture dealers in a provincial saleroom.

When I first joined the firm in 1950, an elderly dealer, who had a shop in Stapleford, Notts, would bring to our saleroom, three piece suites and easy chairs, which he had re-upholstered. He would arrive with the furniture piled high on a trailer behind his car. I knew him as Mr Boden. Since that time we have dealt with his son, Gordon, and then his grandson, Chris.

Chris, who has now retired, was asked, many years ago, by the partners of our firm to join us to be the manager of the mart, a job which he enjoyed and carried out efficiently.

There were usually enough antiques in the monthly furniture sales to attract antique dealers from nearby towns and cities. Local second hand furniture and bric-a-brac dealers in those early years included Andrew Wise of Leicester Street, who insisted that the auctioneer should always knock down any lots he purchased to "Number Four", and Doreen Aldridge, who ran a bric-a-brac shop in Regent Street.

No matter how careful clerks, drovers and farmers are with livestock, with vast numbers of animals passing through the market every week, it is inevitable that, from time to time, some will escape. A few years ago I was walking past the wooded lawns of Crown House, which is situated opposite the cattle market in Scalford Road, when I heard the crowing of a bantam cockerel, which had escaped from the market some weeks previously, and taken up residence among the trees. Here, together with a couple of bantam hens, also market refugees, they were living a sublimely happy life, living on handouts from Inland Revenue employees, which is more than most of us can get. Even more recently there have been two guinea fowl in the same area, these being fed, in specially provided feeding bowls, by some of the customers at the adjacent Co-operative supermarket.

It was more of a problem when a beast escaped from the market. Before the Dr Beeching era, which saw the demise of many minor railway routes, the L.N.E.R. line ran through the rear of the cattle market on top of an embankment. Occasionally beast would escape onto the railway line, and almost before the drovers had scrambled up the embankment, the beast would be well on the way to the village of Scalford, some three miles away, with nothing to impede their gallop. After the closure of the line, the embankment through the market was removed and the ground incorporated into the market.

It was even more serious if a beast escaped and headed into town. Although I cannot recall any serious injury to a member of the public, there have been a few close calls, like the time a fat bullock jumped onto the bonnet of a passing car in Scalford Road. The occupants were not injured, but the car most certainly was.

During the early years in the market, a nervous heifer escaped into Scalford Road and headed towards the town centre, hotly pursued by, but easily outpacing, several drovers. Spotting its own reflection in the plate glass window of Lewis Palmer's furniture store, it charged at the window, cracking it from top to bottom. From there it galloped on through Nottingham Street, scattering stalls and shoppers en route. Looking for an escape route from the frenzied activity around it, the heifer dashed into an alleyway between two shops, turned into a doorway and up a flight of stairs. Its progress was halted by a closed door at the top of the stairs. Behind the door was the small sub office of the "Grantham Journal". Hearing the commotion on the stairs, the reporter quickly opened the door to investigate, but slammed it shut even quicker when confronted by the heifer. There was a story right on the doorstep, but apparently the reporter did not wish to conduct any further investigation at that moment.

The heifer, somehow, managed to extricate itself from the building, and continued its exploration of the town. It was eventually recaptured after demolishing a wall in Albert Street, half a mile from the town centre, and appeared none the worse for its exploits. It had, of course been assured of a report in the next edition of the "Grantham Journal".

Many years ago business between farmers and auctioneers was founded mainly on trust. A practice, which still existed during my early years with the firm, allowed farmers to purchase livestock in the spring and leave the bill unpaid whilst the beast were grazed all summer, and only settled after they had been sold in the autumn. By this time the livestock had grown and was worth considerably more than the purchase price. The firm allowed thousands of pounds worth of credit without charging any interest.

This trust extended to the removal of livestock from the market. For as long as anyone could remember, the usual procedure after the sale was for the purchaser to arrange for the removal of livestock. No checks were ever made to ensure that the correct animals were taken. When a mistake occurred it was rectified fairly quickly. Even so, some buyers could get quite indignant when enquiries were made whilst looking for livestock taken in error, thinking that the finger of suspicion was being pointed in their direction.

However, it became necessary to employ a person to check out store cattle each Tuesday after the sale had finished, after a spate of missing and untraced lots of cattle over a period of several weeks. The culprits, a father and son, from near Hinckley were eventually apprehended by the police, and were trapped by their own incompetence. The pair owned their own cattle lorry, and had replaced the metal ear tags, identifying the cattle, with new ones. This operation was performed in the lorry, but the pair failed to get rid of all the old tags, and police found some of them amongst the straw on the floor of the lorry. The culprits were successfully prosecuted.

'Get out of the ring, Sam!' shouted Martin Shouler, 'You'll get killed one of these days.'

Little Sam Cross had decided to help Lenny, the store cattle ring man, by opening the weighbridge gate for each lot of beast to enter the ring. The steel gate was heavy and stood a lot taller than Sam, who was only a little over five feet tall. Sam was an obliging sort of chap, but because of his diminutive stature, and the fact that he had consumed a few drinks in the market pub, the position was hazardous in the extreme. His reactions were a little slow, and each time he opened the gate, and a beast caught it with its body, the gate flew open and Sam's feet left the ground as he was flung backwards by the impact.

Sam farmed with his brother, Dick, at Upper Broughton, a village about eight miles from Melton. He was a keen horseman and follower of the hunt, but I never saw him drive a vehicle. On market days he would hang around for hours after the auctions were finished until he could hitch a lift home in one of the cattle lorries.

Sam and Dick were seldom seen together in the market. Whenever they were offering store cattle for sale, Dick would keep a low profile at the side of the ring, whilst Sam would follow the beast around the ring shouting their praises and offering some luck money. This must have been an ordeal for Sam, for he would tremble visibly until the beast had been sold.

One week, Sam and Dick were not happy with the trade for three heifers, and decided to take the beast home. Shortly after the auction had ended, I was sitting

in the market office, busy with the usual aftermath of paperwork, when John Brooks, a livestock transporter came over to me.

'Sam Cross has asked me to take his three heifers home, but I can't find them anywhere,' said John.

'O.K., John, I'll come out and have a look,' I said, hoping that they were still in the pens somewhere, and that John had overlooked them. Perhaps another farmer had mistakenly taken them instead of his own beast. Taking the sale sheets with me, I checked all the cattle remaining in the pens, but there was no sign of the three heifers, nor did it appear that the wrong cattle had been taken.

'Well, John,' I said eventually, 'I hope they've not been pinched. I'd better start telephoning around to see if I can trace them.'

John still had more loads of cattle to attend to, so he left me to do whatever I could. Ringing all the purchasers and dealers, to make sure they have the right cattle and the right number of cattle, is a thankless task, and I envisaged a long session on the telephone the following morning. There are always a few buyers who think you are questioning their integrity, and no matter how diplomatic you try to be, things can be rather awkward at times like this.

On this occasion we were lucky. Within ten minutes, John rushed into the office once more. 'Hold everything, Ken, we've found the heifers,' he said.

'Where?' I asked, in disbelief.

'Sam and Dick have messed things up. It's a case of the right hand not knowing what the left hand is doing,' said John, 'I've just been talking to Dick Parker. Apparently Dick Cross asked him to take the beast home, which he's done, but Dick Cross didn't tell his brother, Sam, who in turn asked me to take them. Can you believe it?'

Having seen Dick keeping a low profile outside the ring, and Sam shouting inside the ring, I could well believe it.

The equestrian Melton cross country event was a severe test for horses and riders alike. This popular event was always well supported. Sam Cross was an ardent supporter of the event, for it provided him with the opportunity to combine his love of horses with the chance to socialise and have a few drinks. The trouble with Sam was that he often managed to have one more than he should.

Surrounded by his drinking companions at one event, Sam was soon extolling the virtues of his Aberdeen Angus bull, which was out on hire to John Wiles of Long Clawson, a village about two miles from Sam's farm. After the event was over, Sam insisted that his companions should call to see the bull on the way home. One of his companions was Dick King, cowman to John Wiles. Dick led the way across the crew yard. Sam, who was rather unsteady on his feet, brought up the rear of the group. Suddenly there was a splash and a muffled cry - Sam had fallen head first into a pool of slurry. He had almost submerged before he was pulled out by his laughing companions.

'Come on, Sam, let's get you cleaned up a bit,' said Dick King, the cowman. He grabbed the dairy hosepipe and gave Sam a good hosing down with cold water.

'We'd better get you home now, Sam,' said Dick, 'I'll drive you home in the pick-up.' Sam walked over to the pick-up, his gait decidedly improved by the application of the cold water, and grasped the handle of the passenger door. 'Oh no you don't, Sam, you're not riding in there in that state. Get in the back,' said Dick. Sam meekly obeyed, climbed into the back of the pick-up, sat down on some bags, and was driven the short distance home, still soaking wet.

It had been quite an ordeal for Sam, and was probably more traumatic than anything experienced by any of the riders in the Melton cross country event that day.

The method of getting the information from the many auctions in progress has been the same for over a hundred years. A person was employed to collect the sheets and take them to the market office, where all the relevant information was extracted. This person was known as the sheet runner.

In the case of old Tom Parr, the word "runner" was hardly accurate. Tom, a retired grazier, from Frisby, had done the job for many years, but as old age crept on, he became less capable of maintaining the flow of sheets to the office. It would be fair to say that he could only walk with great difficulty, and with the aid of a walking stick. He had also become quite deaf. On many occasions, Tom would say to me,

'Do you know, Ken, people don't think you're deaf - they think you're daft.'

Despite his mobility difficulties, the partners would never consider relieving him of his position. Somehow, the sheets always got to the office, with Tom only having to walk a short distance. He was such a polite and grateful old gentleman that farmers and clerks regularly came to his assistance.

'Here, Tom, I'm going to the office, I'll take the sheet in for you,' one farmer would say.

'I'll nip and fetch a sheet from the stores for you, Tom,' another farmer would say.

'I'm very grateful to you, thank you kindly,' old Tom would reply.

After a fifty year connection with the market, Tom, then well into his eighties, finally retired, and, in a moving little ceremony in front of the market office, he was presented with a gold watch by the partners.

Nothing could be simpler than taking two sheets from the auction to the office nearby, or so you would think, but life is never that easy.

Len Hewes, the office manager, during nostalgic discussions about his early years with the firm, recalled the Tuesday, early last century, when a sheet, from the sheep auction, failed to arrive at the office. It has always been customary to allow a farmer, who is in a hurry to get home, to take a sheet into the office, as soon as his sheep have been sold, so that he can draw his money and get away quickly. This could happen several times during an auction. Neither the auctioneer nor the clerk could remember who had taken in the sheet. It was assumed that it must have been one of the vendors on that particular sheet, but, by the time the loss had been discovered, most of the farmers had left the market. Most farmers did not have a telephone in those days.

The mystery was solved the following Tuesday, when a farmer, not understanding the system within the market, admitted to having taken the sheet home to show his wife the price realised for his sheep in the auction.

Sixty years ago, a goat was a rare sight in Melton Market. The odd goat which did appear for sale was tethered in the sheep pens and sold at the end of the auction after the rams had been sold.

Gradually, over the next few decades, the numbers increased so much, that a separate auction for goats only was started in a section of the pig shed.

David Willars, who became a partner with Shouler & Son after serving as an articled student with the firm, and gaining his professional qualifications, hated selling goats. 'Put a billy under that pig shed and it stinks to high heaven,' he said, on more than one occasion, so it was with great reluctance that he agreed to sell the goats, one Tuesday, when asked to do so.

The goats were only loosely tethered in the pens, and David and his clerk, walked from pen to pen to sell them. The buyers clustered round the auctioneer and clerk as the sale progressed. When a few pens had been sold, the first sheet had been completed in the booking book. At that moment, Reg Rose, the sheet runner, appeared on the far side of the pen, and motioned to David that he wanted a sheet. David took the completed sheet from his clerk, leant across the pen, and proffered the sheet to Reg.

Suddenly, and with lightning speed, a hungry goat snatched the sheet from David's hand, and devoured it at an alarming rate. Despite willing hands attempting to prise open the goat's jaws to retrieve the sheet, with one final gulp, the sheet was despatched forever.

It took a long time to decide what the prices on the sheet had been. It is remarkable how the vendors and purchasers can differ when faced with such a memory test. Eventually, all was resolved, and the remaining goats were sold without incident, but David's aversion to selling goats was even stronger.

During the fifties, with the development of larger lorries, a welcome addition to the revenue of the market developed, and has flourished ever since. This was the appearance of loads of fodder for sale in the market. During the peak periods there were forty to fifty loads each Tuesday. Initially, the loads were placed alongside the pens and sheds in the centre of the market, continuing along the roadway out of the rear of the market and on to the car park. There were so many loads arriving that, eventually, a special fodder park was allocated to accommodate all the lorries.

Every kind of fodder was on display, from hay and straw to mangolds and feed potatoes. Every load had been over a public weighbridge and the driver would hand the weigh ticket to the auctioneer. After the auction, loads would be delivered to the purchaser's farm by the vendor free of charge up to ten miles, thereafter a charge of half a crown for each mile in excess was imposed. Sometimes the fodder would be sold by sample, with a couple of bales only on display to show the quality. The vendor would then agree to supply a load based on the sample of up to ten tons of the bales.

For a number of years, John Burgin, the fat sheep auctioneer, sold the fodder after the conclusion of the sheep auction. One Tuesday he was attempting to sell a load of hay by sample. The weather had been mild and there was little interest in the two sample bales.

Only a few farmers stood clustered round the two bales, and most of them were simply curious. As there was a reserve price on the hay, John started off the bidding and trotted up towards the reserve price. There were no bidders around him, and he was just about to buy the lot in, when there was a shout from a man who had just appeared on the scene. The hay was knocked down to this newcomer and John immediately asked him how many tons he would like delivered. The man looked aghast, turned on his heel, and ran off before John could even ask him his name. He obviously thought that John was selling just the two bales, and had taken fright at the mere mention of the word "tons".

The man probably kept just a few rabbits.

CHAPTER TWELVE

Land drainage surveys

I surveyed with Mark,
Who was up for a lark.
We measured in muck
When farmers were stuck,
And were desperate to plough,
But we managed somehow.
From the hills and the vales
Come many more tales.

After the second world war the firm was involved in surveying land drainage schemes for farmers, and preparing plans of those schemes on linen. During the fifties and sixties, a generous government grant was available towards the cost of those schemes, and at one stage reached a high of sixty per cent of the cost.

For each application, a proposed scheme was designed by the Ministry drainage officer, and a working plan was drawn showing the approximate drain positions. This was used by the drainage contractor, and closely followed when the actual drains were laid. After completion of the scheme, we would conduct a survey, plot the actual positions of the drains, and draw an accurate plan on linen, which was one of the government requirements before any grant could be paid. It was claimed that draining wet land improved productivity by ten per cent.

We were, at one stage, carrying out surveys for seven contractors. The three main contractors in the local area were John Cook, Richard Ingham, and Peter Drewry. Peter traded as "Saxby Drainage." Norman Fowler and I carried out the surveys during the early years. Norman, a farmer's son, was my age, and newly qualified.

It was a raw November day when we surveyed a scheme below the woods at Little Dalby. It had rained heavily the day before, and the mud was thick and heavy. After a couple of hours struggling through the mud, which clung to the tape along the whole hundred feet length, we were feeling tired.

'Let's stop for a breather,' said Norman, as he scraped the mud off the tape to read the measurement. I was only too happy to agree, so we left the tape lying in the mud, and took refuge from the biting wind against a tall hedgerow.

As we stood and smoked our cigarettes, the autumn leaves fluttered down around us. The whole landscape was beginning to assume its winter cloak. The tranquillity of our surroundings was interrupted suddenly by the sound of a hunting horn, and, within a few minutes, we were surrounded by hounds and huntsmen. As one of the huntsmen rode alongside the hedgerow towards us, Norman spotted a fox slip out of a wood and run across an adjacent field.

'There goes your fox!' he shouted excitedly to the approaching huntsman.

'We don't want *that* bloody fox,' sneered the huntsman, icily. The huntsman rode off leaving a rather crestfallen Norman to ponder. The huntsman could have been more civil and his attitude did nothing to further the sport of foxhunting. I know that this encounter left Norman unimpressed with the sport, but I am not sure whether it changed his views in the long term.

Some weeks later we again encountered the hunt. One of the followers, a young man in mud spattered riding habit, pulled up his horse close to us as we measured in the mud. He watched us for a few minutes before he spoke.

'I say, chaps, I'm going to be a chartered surveyor, but if this is what they have to do, I must say I'm not very keen,' he drawled.

Norman looked at me. He had no need to say what he thought, for I could read it in his expression. We carried on with our work, and the young man wheeled his horse around and rode off.

Norman and I spent many happy hours surveying land drainage schemes. We were out in all kinds of weather, often conversing and shouting out the measurements in German, which we had both studied at school. The time came, however, when Norman had to concentrate on other aspects of the business, and I was left to continue the surveying with the assistance of the junior clerk in the office.

When Mark Seymour joined the firm as junior clerk, he soon gained a reputation as a prankster. It was Mark who slipped the rubber imitation chocolate biscuit onto Len Hewes' saucer one morning, then rolled about laughing as Len initially tried to lick off some chocolate, then attempted to bite it. It was Mark who smeared ink on the brass door knob to my office just before I opened the door, but it wasn't long before he had to show that he, too, could take a joke.

Like all office juniors before him, Mark had to spend part of his time working in the mart, and be in attendance on furniture sale viewing days. Some prospective purchasers, who could not attend the auction, would never leave their commissions to buy with the auctioneers, preferring instead to entrust the bidding to one of the porters or clerks.

One local businessman, who owned a vintage vehicle museum, was interested in a penny farthing bicycle, which was entered in the next sale. On the viewing day he left a commission with Mark to bid up to a hundred pounds for the bicycle.

Only a few weeks prior to this, porters and clerks had been warned by the partners that persons carrying out these commissions may well be held responsible for the debt should the purchaser not pay for the goods. This warning followed one or two instances of debts occurring in this way. Nevertheless, the practice continued.

On the day of the sale, Mark was working behind the rostrum finding the items for sale. Meanwhile, the girls in the office, who had often been on the receiving end of Mark's pranks, were now plotting against him. One of the girls slipped, unobtrusively, into the mart, just prior to the bicycle being offered, and watched whilst the lot was sold. After ensuring that Mark had bought the lot, she returned quickly to the office and scribbled a note, supposedly a telephone message from the businessman, instructing Mark not to buy the penny farthing as he had now changed his mind. The note was sent, via one of the porters, to the mart and handed to Mark.

The reaction was not long in arriving. Barely two minutes later, Mark dashed into the office. His face was pale and drawn.

'When did he phone? What did he say? What am I supposed to do now?' he gasped, not waiting for any answers. His mind was preoccupied with the thought of paying out a hundred pounds for the penny farthing.

The girls were finding it difficult to keep straight faces, but they held out for a few minutes before coming clean and putting him out of his misery.

'You rotten devils !' said Mark, his voice almost a whisper, but gradually a grin spread across his face as he recovered his composure, and he was soon chatting away happily to the girls, discussing the possibility of a good tip from the businessman for buying the penny farthing. 'I reckon I might get a fiver from him,' he said finally before returning to the mart.

A few days later, the businessman called at the office to pay his bill and collect the bicycle. Mark accompanied him to the mart to assist with the loading. On his return, the girls were eager to find out much Mark had received as a tip.

'Show us this fiver then, Mark' they chorused.

'He's a bit tighter than I thought,' said Mark, disconsolately, 'He's given me two complimentary tickets to visit his museum the next time I'm in Norfolk.'

The expectation of receiving a tip for an extra service rendered was prevalent in many areas of working lives, none more so than in the saleroom and the cattle market. Every sale day or market day a few coins would change hands for some small service rendered. A porter would buy lots for an antique dealer who could not attend the sale, or assist with loading furniture onto a vehicle. In the cattle market there were many ways for a clerk or drover to "earn a shilling."

It was on the last Tuesday before Christmas that the cattle dealers were particularly generous towards the clerk and drovers, and was eagerly anticipated as that day approached. It was at Christmas, too, that the land drainage contractors showed their appreciation. Usually I would receive a bottle of whisky or wine from some of them.

One Christmas I did not receive the usual bottle from Saxby Drainage, but a year later, when I returned to the office after a day in the fields, I was surprised to find three bottles of the finest Scotch whisky on my desk. Each bottle had a gift label and each one was signed by Peter Drewry and each bore a different message. The first one read "This one is for last Xmas because we forgot." The second one read "This one is for this Xmas." The last one read "This one is for next Xmas in case we forget again" Sentiments that were greatly appreciated by family and relations that Xmas - even more so after we had sampled that whisky.

It was always a great feeling to get out of the office and into the fields, particularly on a fine summer's day. Mark reclined the passenger seat and stretched out his tall frame as we headed out of town and into the undulating and beautiful countryside of Leicestershire. It was nine thirty, and already we could see that it was going to be a hot day. It had rained heavily the previous day, but now there was not a cloud to be seen.

We rarely called at the farmhouse, as we usually had a working sketch plan of the scheme, given to us by the drainage contractor. This enabled us to go straight to the field, thus saving a lot of time.

When we arrived at the nearest point to the field, I parked the car on the grass verge. We pulled on our wellingtons, picked up the surveying equipment, and set off across the three fields to the scheme. It was getting hotter by the minute.

'I don't know about you, but I'm taking my shirt off today,' said Mark, peeling it off as he spoke.

'Not a bad idea, Mark,' I replied, and did likewise. 'We'd better not leave them in this field though - look, there's some beast at the far end of the field.'

We climbed the fence into the field where the drainage scheme had been laid, and decided to leave our shirts on top of a low hedge on one side of the field, and well out of reach of the beast in the adjoining field. The field containing the scheme was L-shaped, and, as we surveyed the scheme, we gradually turned the corner so that, by the time we had finished, some two hours later, we were well out of sight of our starting point. We had completed the survey in good time. The muddy puddles, a reminder of the previous day's rain, were drying up rapidly. We stood for a few minutes and studied the measurements we had taken to ensure we had not missed any vital ties.

When we were satisfied that nothing was amiss we reeled in the tape and set off across the field towards our starting point. As we walked and chatted, comparing the first signs of this year's sun tans, we were unprepared for the sight which met our eyes as we turned the corner.

'Oh! No! Look at that,' exclaimed Mark, 'The bloody cows have got our shirts.'

Whilst we were out of sight at the far end of the field, the farmer had opened a gate in the corner of the field to allow his milking herd access to the grazing between the filled-in drains. The ever curious cows had pulled our shirts from the hedge and dragged them through some muddy patches. We retrieved the shirts and found that

the sun had dried out the mixture of water, mud and saliva, and we were able to put on the shirts, but when we returned to the office, we looked more like tramps than surveyors.

The more I worked among cattle, the more I discovered about their curiosity, and their inclinations, but there was usually a price to pay for the knowledge gained.

I had just taken delivery of a new car - a fresh car would be more correct as I had never had a new car. The car was clean and sparkling from a wash and polish on the Sunday, and now, on Monday morning, it was purring its way through the countryside, past the woods on Dalby top, around the top of the escarpment, beneath which the lovely Vale of Belvoir stretched as far as the eye could see.

The drainage scheme was in a field on the side of the escarpment, near Old Dalby, and three fields back from the road. There was a cart track across to the field so I was able to leave the car in the field adjacent to the one with the drainage scheme. Whilst pulling on my Wellies, I spotted a herd of Friesian cows at the far end of the field, but it was the wrong time of year for sun bathing, so I was not unduly concerned about the cows.

As we climbed the fence into the field with the scheme, a glorious sight met our eyes. Between the lines of the drains stretching across the grass field, were hundreds of mushrooms. Normally I would have had to search high and low to find a mushroom patch and then, probably, found only a few mushrooms at a time. Here they were everywhere, big ones, small ones, some past their best, and some just pushing through the grass, the rich rewards of a warm and humid night.

The survey was delayed whilst I dashed back to the car to fetch a couple of carrier bags, which I always carried for occasions such as this. We filled the bags within minutes, and stowed them away in the boot of the car. We were still congratulating ourselves on our good fortune as we started surveying the scheme. Two hours later the job was done, the tape reeled in, and we were climbing the fence on the way to the car. The cows were all at the far end of the field, but as we walked towards the car, I thought it looked different somehow, but I couldn't quite put my finger on the difference until we were much closer. The cows had been at my possessions again. The windows and paintwork were smeared all over, where the cows had licked and rubbed against the car, and the radio aerial had been snapped off. The delight at the discovery of the mushrooms had been somewhat dampened by this latest bovine encounter.

After the experiences with the car and the cows, I was careful not to leave the car in any field in which cattle were grazing, so when Mark and I arrived at Gunthorpe Hall, near Oakham, to survey a drainage scheme, I made certain there was no danger of a repeat performance.

Dick Matthews, the farm manager, had telephoned our office before the scheme had been completed, wanting to know when we could carry out the survey.

'Richard Ingham will be finished tomorrow morning, and I want to get in with the plough,' he said.

'All right, Dick, we'll pull your scheme in tomorrow afternoon,' I promised, knowing how desperate farmers were to get the crop sown and established before the advent of winter.

As we walked towards the scheme the autumn ploughing was in progress in nearby fields. The roar of the tractors mingled with the screeching of hundreds of gulls, wheeling and swooping behind the plough. They squabbled and fought for the tasty morsels unearthed by the plough.

It was a bright, crisp day, and there was a distinct nip in the air. We were soon on the move to keep warm. It was a straightforward scheme - one long, straight main drain ran parallel and close to the hedge, with a dozen lateral drains running across the field into the main drain. When we were halfway through the scheme we took a short break. It was the time of year for us to sample some of Mother Nature's provisions, and we spent a few minutes feasting on blackberries, which were growing in abundance on the south facing hedgerow.

After the last measurement had been taken and all checks made, we returned to the car, safe in the knowledge that no beast could get near it, so, once again, we were totally unprepared for the sight which met our eyes. The car was almost completely covered in bird droppings. It seemed as though the gulls, gorged from the rich pickings behind the plough, had targeted my car for dive bombing practice. The windscreen was so thickly covered that it took several minutes to clear it sufficiently to be able to drive safely. At that moment, I really believed my car was ill fated.

During the peak years for land drainage, when the government subsidy was at an all- time high, we were carrying out surveys for several contractors. The contractors were laying drains so quickly that it became more difficult to keep up to date with the surveys. Not only did we have to take all the measurements, but we also had to plot the schemes and produce a certified plan on linen, which the farmer sent in to the Ministry of Agriculture in order to obtain the grant.

Hardly an evening passed without a telephone call from one of the contractors.

'Hello, Ken, John Cook here. I've just finished a hundred chains at Sileby. When can you fit it in?'

'Well, John, I'm just doing a big scheme for Saxby Drainage at the moment, and then I've got a small scheme to measure at Gaddesby for Richard Ingham. It might be Friday morning before I get to yours.'

'Don't leave it too long. The farmer says he is going to spread chicken muck on it in the next few days.'

These were the words I dreaded most. There were many farmers who did not realise how difficult they made our job when they spread muck on the field or started to plough before the survey had been carried out. One or two farmers were so uninformed that they had ploughed up the whole field before we arrived. This meant that we then had to spend valuable time probing to find the location of the drains before we could even start the survey. Despite providing us with all these headaches, the farmers still expected us to provide that invaluable plan, without which they could not obtain that all important grant.

Dry, well-rotted manure was not too bad. Chicken muck was slippery and evil smelling, but worst of all was manure slurry.

One day I took my younger son, Paul with me to survey a scheme in Tickencote field, some way down the Great North Road. The field was the site of a battle between the Royalists and Parliamentarians during the 17th century civil war, and was marked as such on the Ordnance Survey plan of the area.

When we arrived I saw that it was a stubble field, and the drains, which were neatly filled in, were laid in a straightforward pattern. We donned our old coats, pulled on our wellingtons, and were soon absorbed in measuring the scheme at one end of the field. We had worked our way across the field to a point just over halfway, when, suddenly, with a mighty roar, a huge tractor and slurry spreader swung into the field behind us, and tore across the field slinging manure slurry in all directions. The driver sat high and dry in his enclosed cab, but still felt the need to wear a mask over his mouth and nose - a sure indication of the toxic nature of the slurry he would be slinging in our direction if we didn't get out quickly.

I decided, as the tractor returned to the farm for the next load, that we would take the minimum number of measurements necessary to be able to plot the scheme. This we did, and got out before we were felled by the slurry, as so many were felled by other weapons in Tickencote field a long time ago.

Paul assisted me too when we surveyed a drainage scheme at Moscow Farm, Little Dalby. The farm nestled at the foot of the escarpment which carried at its summit the iron- age encampment known as Burrough Hill. The farm was owned by the Johnson family and the buildings were strung out some distance alongside the road. As the scheme to be surveyed lay directly behind the farm I decided to park the car at the farm. As we got out of the car one of the Johnson brothers rode up to us on a bicycle. He pointed out to us the easiest route to the field, but as he spoke I was staring at his bicycle.

'I see you only have the right hand side of the handlebars. What happened to the left side?' I said

'It kept getting in the way of everything so I took it off', he replied. 'Because the buildings are so spread out I need the cycle for expediency, and it's surprising the things I can carry now the handlebar doesn't get in the way. I've still got a brake on the right side.'

We took our leave and walked towards the field on the hill behind the farm, still musing about the ingenuity of some farmers. The scheme had been laid in a pasture field and grazing the field were some twenty or more young bulls. These bulls were about a year old. They had been reared together so they didn't fight amongst themselves, and they were being fattened for meat. We each took a stout stick in case of any problems as we measured. There were none on this occasion, but the bulls had just developed that deep rumbling roar of the male bovine, and it was rather disconcerting to suddenly hear that roar close behind you as you measured. I was more than a little relieved to finish the scheme, and I believe Paul was too.

Mark and I would often walk several miles during the course of a day's work. It was often a hard slog, particularly during the winter months, but we loved to be out in the fields, and we did have our lighter moments.

Mark was a compulsive prankster, and one of his favourite tricks was his "disappearing act". Tie measurements to a hedge line were always taken from the hedge roots, and this often entailed one of us jumping down into a ditch to be able to reach them with the end of the tape. Mark would jump into the ditch, raise his hands in the air, whilst slowly bending his knees, and, as he gradually disappeared from sight below the top edge of the ditch, he would shout 'Help.' From a hundred feet away, at the other end of the tape, it looked as though he had jumped into a bog and was sinking fast.

The first time he pulled the trick I dashed over wondering what was amiss, but thereafter the joke wore a little thin, and one day his little prank rather backfired on him.

We were surveying a scheme and at one point Mark had to cross a dried up pond in the corner of the field to take a tie measurement. I watched from the other end of the tape as he jumped down into the pond, and, true to form, his hands went up with a cry for help.

'Oh! No! Not again!' I shouted, 'That joke's wearing a bit thin.'

'I'm serious - I'm sinking,' he yelled back.

'Pull the other one, come on, Mark, stop messing about.'

I paused and lit a cigarette before strolling over towards him. I fully expected him to shout 'Fooled you again,' but he didn't. When I reached the pond I could see why. He was stuck fast in slimy black mud, which was oozing close to the tops of his wellingtons. The thin layer of dried cracked mud had been concealing something more sinister. I started to laugh.

'Don't mess about - get me out,' he pleaded.

I savoured the moment, 'I can see the farm a couple of fields away. I'll just pop over to borrow a rope,' I said, jokingly.

'Oh come on ! - I'm stuck fast - I can't move,' he said.

Before the mud could enter his wellingtons, I managed to extricate him with the aid of a long branch. Mark never repeated his disappearing act after that incident.

By working in the cattle market, I got to know many farmers by sight and by name, but there are always some whose faces you recognise, but whose names escape you.

There were also some farmers, whose names were familiar through booking, but whom you had not actually met.

I had never met Vernon Towle, but I had written his name scores of times, so when Richard Ingham rang me one evening to tell me there was a completed scheme ready for surveying at Vernon Towle's farm, I knew that we would be heading for Walton on the Wolds, a village near Loughborough.

A working plan of the scheme awaited me at the office the following morning, so we could go straight to the field and get on with the job. The field lay close to the farm, so it was convenient to leave the car in the farmyard, well away from the mouths of curious cattle, although I could see some young black and white Hereford cross heifers in the field we were about to survey in.

Young cattle, in particular, are curious, and, as we took the first measurements, one or two of the heifers were nosing at the tape, then dashing away as we flicked the tape upwards again, only to cautiously approach once more. As Mark and I proceeded along the main drain, the spring sunshine warming our backs, the heifers appeared to lose interest and returned to their grazing.

We were soon engrossed in our work, and soon reached the bottom end of the gently sloping field. Here we paused and stood together to study the plan and decide the strategy for the rest of the survey.

One end of the tape was in my hand holding the clipboard, whilst the rest of the tape trailed behind us in the grass. As we stood preoccupied with our study of the working plan, I felt a sudden jerk on the tape, which almost knocked the board from my grasp. We spun round only to see, to our dismay, the other end of the tape slowly disappearing into the mouth of one of the heifers.

'Quick - pull it out,' shouted Mark.

I gave the tape a sharp tug, but the tape snapped. I quickly gathered in the tape and when we examined it, we found that the heifer had swallowed five feet off the end. The tape was made of a plastic material known as "fibron". Ironically, there was, at that time a "keep the countryside free of plastic rubbish" campaign, in which the dangers to farm animals from plastic rubbish were highlighted. This campaign immediately sprang to mind, and I had visions of a vet carrying out a post mortem on this heifer, and solemnly pulling out the five feet of tape in much the same way a magician might pull a string of flags from his mouth.

There was another difficulty. The six heifers in the field looked identical.

'Keep your eye on the one that swallowed the tape,' I said to Mark, as I looked round trying to think of something constructive to do. I spotted a farm worker busy singling with a hoe in the adjoining field.

'Excuse me,' I shouted, 'Do you think you could spare a minute to help us?'

The man looked up from his labours, and leaned heavily on the top of his hoe with both hands. 'What's the trouble Mister?' he asked.

'One of these heifers has just swallowed five feet off the end of our plastic tape, and I wondered if you knew where Mr Towle was, so that I could have a word with him. He really ought to keep an eye on the heifer.'

The man slowly rolled up his sagging shirt sleeves, then climbed over the fence to join us. 'Hmmm, swallowed five feet off your tape, did she?' he mused, 'Don't sound too good.'

'No, I don't think it's that serious. It should pass through her system, but he ought to keep an eye on her,' I said, hoping he would agree.

'I dunno, I've seen 'em die o' less things than that,' he said shaking his head gravely.

'I really think I should have a word with Mr Towle. Do you know where he is?' I asked again.

'The gaffer won't be back till tea time,' said the man, leaning heavily on his hoe once more, 'Which is the heifer?'

'It's the one on the right of the bunch,' said Mark, who had been keeping the heifers under close observation.

'Hmmm, just as I thought, she's the best o' the bunch, an' wi' trade for stores as it is, she'd be worth quite a bit, an' if she dies you'll be responsible,' said the man, almost gleefully.

I looked at the ruddy faced, middle aged farm worker. It seemed as if he was enjoying the unease I was obviously displaying. He continued to expound about store cattle prices and trends in other market departments, and it was at that point that I began to suspect that all was not as it seemed. For a farm worker, this man had an unusual depth of knowledge about prices and trends.

'By the way,' I said, changing the subject quickly, 'when your gaffer gets back, tell him he may not get the grant on this scheme.'

The grin suddenly left the man's face, 'Why? What do you mean? What's the problem?' he asked. His mouth had dropped open, and he bore a worried look.

'Well, he's put in a drain from the ditch, near that corner over there, to the main drain of this scheme, and it's against Ministry regulations,' I said, trying hard to sound stern.

The man was forced into the open. He smiled and held out his hand, 'I'm Vernon Towle - that heifer will be just fine. Shall we talk about the ditch?'

I smiled and shook his hand. 'Why not indeed?' I said.

Whenever I met Vernon in the cattle market in the years that followed, and sampled one of the Fox's glacier mints, which he invariably carried in his pocket, we would always share a laugh about the day the heifer swallowed the tape.

Junior members of staff came and went, some within months of starting. One lad, on his first scheme as my assistant, became so ill during the survey that operations had to be suspended, and I drove him back to the office. The scheme was in a meadow, the pollen count must have been high, the poor lad's eyes were streaming, and he could not stop sneezing. I had no alternative but to take him back to the office, where he soon recovered.

There came a time when no-one from within the office could assist me on the surveys, so I was forced to obtain assistance from elsewhere. Tony Stevenson, a neighbour, and Ken Elsom, a shift worker, helped me for some time. Kevin Collier, a policeman, who subsequently left the force to buy a smallholding in Wales, also helped. Kevin had led a varied life, and I always found his tales fascinating.

My three children also took turns to hold the end of the tape, and on one occasion, my wife, Margaret, also donned her old clothes to help me.

This time, we had a longer trip than usual. The scheme was near Desford, and, as I always avoided driving through Leicester if I could, we took the country route. The scheme was in a roadside field close to a wood, and I was able to park the car in a nearby lay-by. I pulled on my wellingtons, and Margaret put on an old pair of fur lined boots she had brought along for the occasion.

It was a straightforward scheme, which didn't take long to survey. When we arrived back at the car, the tape was stowed away in the boot, and we changed back into our shoes. It was not until we arrived home that we made the awful discovery. Still standing, in a lay-by near Desford, was one pair of fur lined boots. It would have been far too costly to retrieve them, so they may still be standing there to this day. I suspect that there have been many guesses at the probable fate of the owner.

The government grant on drainage schemes was eventually reduced, and soon after it was further reduced. Not so many schemes were being carried out, and I decided that I could survey them without any assistance. I attached a steel peg (to push into the ground) to one end of the tape, whilst I took the measurements. It was a slower process, but it worked.

I was coping well surveying the drainage schemes without an assistant, and surveying the scheme for Andy Holland, whose family have farmed at Twyford for over four hundred years, was to be yet another solo effort. The scheme was in a field, well out of the village, along the road to Ashby Folville. When I arrived, I left the car in the roadside field. After so many brushes with cattle in the past, my first instinct was to scan the field to see if there was any livestock. Some farm buildings and an open yard stood at one end of the field. I walked over to the buildings. Contained within the yard were five large

Friesian bullocks, the breed favoured by Andy and often sold in the store cattle auction at Melton market. If they got near the car they would give it a good licking and buffeting.

Satisfied that the car was safe from the attention of curious cattle, I crossed over the brook to begin measuring the drainage scheme. Although we were well into autumn, we were enjoying a few warm days. Shortly after I began, Andy arrived on a tractor to start ploughing an adjoining field. A few minutes later, I noticed, to my horror, that my car was now surrounded by the Friesian bullocks. On his way, Andy had stopped to let the cattle out of the yard to take advantage of the warm weather and the grass.

I dashed back to the car to move it out of the field, but, to my utter dismay, I realised that the car keys were still in the ignition, and I had closed the door with the lock on. Noticing my frantic efforts to keep the beast away from the car, Andy came over, and we shepherded the beast back into the yard and fastened the gate.

I then had a long walk, in my Wellingtons, into the village to make a phone call from Andy's farmhouse to the office in Melton. From there a colleague had to drive to my house to collect a spare set of car keys from my wife, and then bring them out to Twyford. After completing the survey, and whilst I awaited my colleague's arrival, I leant against the car with my elbows on the roof, chin resting in cupped hands, and I am sure I heard my car whisper 'Thank you.'

CHAPTER THIRTEEN

White Hart & VAT

Tales about quarterly VAT,
And a genial landlord called Pat.
From Galway he came,
And made quite a name.
There's also the tale
Of a collie for sale.
When the police made a call
There was nowt left at all !

Tramping up and down fields all day was thirsty work, especially during the summer months, and a visit to "The White Hart" in Melton, during the evenings, to enjoy a pint or two of Marston's Pedigree bitter, was always a welcome sojourn.

"The White Hart" was a popular pub, and was dubbed "The Irish Embassy" by many locals, as it was frequented by many of the local Irish community, and the landlord, Pat Lohan, hailed from Galway. Pat was a most genial Irishman, who had that enviable knack of making his customers feel at ease. For twenty years he ran the pub, together with his wife Beryl, and it was a sad day when they called "time gentlemen please" for the last time at "The White Hart". However, during that twenty years, the pub was to prove to be one of the most popular in town. It was not a pub with plush seating and surroundings, and, although quite a few women could be seen there, I always had the feeling that the venue was chosen by the men. It was deemed to be more of a man's pub, with Guiness, Lager and Marston's Pedigree all on draught. It also became the local for several officers of the police force. Like the cows at milking time, all the regulars would sit or stand in the same places. Whenever I called in for a pint, I would stand "round the corner" as it was known. Here, at different times, with an old school friend, Alf Andow, John Watson, a local farmer, my two brothers, Ray and Jeff, and two more friends Robin Welbourn and Phil Creed, we would solve all the world's problems, and run this country far better than any government had done so far - particularly after we had enjoyed a couple of pints!

'Hallo, Ken, how's she cutten?' asked Pat one evening when I walked in. This turn of phrase puzzled me, and Pat had to explain that it was a greeting, commonly used during his boyhood years, among farmers back in Galway, and had derived from the banter between farmers when the hay was mown. Pat often greets me in the same way now.

Shortly after taking over "The White Hart", Pat bought a bungalow, with a few acres of land and some farm sheds, close to the river Eye, which flows through Melton. Here he kept chickens, fattened pigs, and reared a few beast each year. Eventually, the customers at the pub, in addition to buying a pint, could also buy a dozen free range eggs, and take home the occasional joint of pork. The carcass each time was expertly jointed by Ivan Thompson, a local butcher, and was on display in the skittle alley at the rear of the pub.

When value added tax was introduced in the early seventies, Pat asked me if I would calculate his liability, and fill in his V.A.T. return each quarter. I agreed, and did it for the next twenty years for the duration of Pat's tenancy. I was soon persuaded to perform his annual stocktaking, and when one of his daughters, Judy, took on the Post Office and grocery store on Thorpe Road, I was likewise involved. After this, Pat bought an off-licence on Thorpe Road, which again required four V.A.T. returns and one stocktaking a year. Finally, he acquired the corner store on Saxby Road, which his son, Chris, was to run for many years. Once again, I had another part-time job four times a year.

When Pat built his own house, he used the talents of the tradesmen who frequented the pub, and whenever a bricklayer, plumber, or carpenter had some spare time they would be working on Pat's new house. When it was finally completed, I obtained a rebate of all the V.A.T. paid on the materials. That ensured me a few free pints during the following weeks.

During Pat's time at the pub, there were both men's and ladies' darts and skittles teams. There were outings to the seaside, and visits to the brewery. At one time there was live music one night a week. At Sunday lunchtimes, there would always be free, hot, cocktail sausage rolls to nibble at, and at Christmas there were free pints for the regulars.

Pat's smallholding was affectionately known as "The Ponderosa" after the popular television series, "Bonanza", and, occasionally, Pat would hold parties there for his regulars, with music and dancing in a barn. He was a popular landlord.

When Eric Turner, who enjoyed his pint at the Hart, took over the fruit and veg. shop from his brother, Aly, he asked me if I would keep his books and deal with his V.A.T. Once more, I agreed, and did them for several years.

Periodically, the books would be subject to examination by Customs and Excise. When that day arrived it was arranged that the scrutiny should take place in the lounge at Eric's house, as there was no suitable room at the lock-up shop. As I had kept the books, I naturally agreed to attend the meeting.

The books were relatively simple, and after an hour or so the visit was almost at an end. The Customs and Excise officer picked up his briefcase and turned to Eric,

'Before I go I would like to see your final balance sheets, which your accountant provided for you last year.'

'Oh, they're in my briefcase in the shop,' said Eric, 'I'll fetch them. I shall only be a few minutes.' With that, he slipped on his jacket and left the house.

The officer and I indulged in small talk for five minutes, then another five, and still there was no sign of Eric. After twenty minutes, the officer glanced anxiously at his watch, 'I think I had better be off now,' he said, 'I can see the balance sheets another day.' He took his leave and departed.

I knew that the quickest route to Eric's shop, from his house, was along two streets, and in through the rear entrance of the "White Hart", through the building and out the front door, where his shop was situated only a few yards away. I took this route too, as I was ready for a pint, and I had a shrewd idea that the mystery would soon be solved. Sure enough, when I walked into the pub, I spotted Eric sitting at a table in the corner, nonchalantly sipping his pint.

'What happened, couldn't you find them?' I asked.

'No, I didn't bother looking,' he said, 'I knew you could deal with him.'

I was flabbergasted. I had never encountered such a cavalier attitude towards authority. I suppose, upon reflection, he had just paid me a backhanded compliment. What more could I say - at least he bought me a pint!

During this twenty year period, I kept the books for various small businessmen in my spare time. One of these was Graham Wilkinson, who ran a small plumbing business. Graham, with his wife Judy and their two young sons, lived not fifty yards from my house.

At the end of each financial quarter, he would provide me with all his bills, cheque stubs, and all the necessary information to complete his quarterly accounts and to calculate his V.A.T. liability.

One summer, after returning from a summer holiday, I telephoned Graham to remind him that his quarter had ended, and that his V.A.T. return was due within two weeks. Graham was rather surprised.

'I sent one of the lads round with all the things in a carrier bag - let's see - it would be just over a week ago.'

'That's strange,' I said, 'I've not seen anything around the house. Ask him where he left the bag, and let me know.'

The next day, Graham called to tell me that when his son had brought the bag round, he found no-one at home so he leant the bag against the dustbin, which was close to the rear door. The awful realisation hit us both simultaneously. The refuse collectors had taken a whole quarter's bills, cheque stubs, bank statements, and much more whilst we were on holiday.

When Graham rang Customs and Excise to explain, they were not impressed. "A likely story" would best summarise their reaction. They proceeded to assess his liability for that quarter, which would adjust naturally when the true figures were ascertained the following quarter. Before this, however, came the time consuming task of obtaining duplicates of every piece of paperwork involved. No bag was ever left outside again.

One of my responsibilities was the V.A.T. liability calculations and payment for various clients of the firm. This gave me an insight into many different aspects of the tax, so it was no surprise when Martin asked me to pop over to see Mike Loxton of Leesthorpe, and deal with a claim for him.

Mike was an amiable chap, and easy to talk to. Pigs were his main source of income, and he had just built a large new pig unit containing pens, creep feeds and so on, for his stock. He was allowed to claim back the V.A.T. on all materials, even the concrete, used in the construction. This was just one of the many varied tasks carried out by the firm.

Apart from the land drainage schemes, many of the smaller surveying jobs also fell within my remit. These included surveying and drawing up plans of houses and gardens, division of fields and calculation of the new acreages, and many similar jobs.

One Monday I had to survey a small field near Knossington. The field had been a council tip site, which had been filled and grassed over. It was now being offered for sale by tender by the local authority. A lady, who was interested in purchasing the field, had asked us to check the acreage, as she thought that there were less than the three acres advertised.

As I drove towards Knossington, I could feel the cruel north westerly wind buffeting the car. In front, a pair of carrion crows, flying close to the ground, rose to clear a hedge, only to stall above the hedge as they battled against the wind, then falling back before succeeding at the second attempt.

When I pulled into the lay-by, where large skips had replaced the former tip site, and got out of the car, the wind was making the telephone wires sing, and plastic bags, sucked up from the nearby rubbish, were flapping away in protest at being caught up in the hedgerow.

As I pulled on my wellingtons, and turned up the collar of my coat to fend off the biting wind, I spotted the tall, lean figure of Charlie Broome, a local farmer I had known for years, straighten up from against a skip. I hadn't noticed him before, as he had been rummaging, head down, inside one of the skips. When he emerged, he held aloft the handles off an old lawnmower, and an elbow joint for a drainpipe. He walked across the road and threw them over a hedge into a field, obviously to retrieve them at a later date. I was mystified over the intended use of the lawnmower handles, but my thoughts were interrupted by the arrival of a council lorry. The driver and his mate climbed from the cab and sauntered over to where I stood. As I took the clip board and tape out of the boot, the two middle-aged council men stood and stared. They were wondering what I was going to do. The lorry driver spoke first.

'Are you from the council surveyor's department?' he asked.

'No, a private firm,' I replied, 'I've just got to check the area of the old tip site.'

Charlie walked over and joined the other two men, and we stood for a while discussing the merits of a field with little topsoil and a subsoil of old bottles and cans, and the possible uses for such a field, when suddenly the driver changed the subject to tell us of an accident he had witnessed the previous day on the Great North Road, near the "Ram Jam Inn". The mention of this particular inn seemed to jog old Charlie's memory, and he rubbed his chin thoughtfully.

'I've only been inside the "Ram Jam" once in my life,' he said, 'And I'll tell you why.' Turning towards me, he continued, 'Do you remember Holvey's farm sale at Owston, a few years back?'

'Yes, I do Charlie,' I replied.

'Well, I thought I would nip over and see if there were 'owt going a bit cheap, and I took me Collie bitch wi' me,' he said, motioning to the dog which now lay, patiently, head resting on paws, at his feet. 'While I was there, I got talking to this feller, and he said to me,

'That's a good bitch you got there mister.'

'Aye, she is a good bitch,' I said, 'And a good worker.'

'You wouldn't sell her, I suppose?' the feller asked me.

'I might - and I've got her two brothers at home, and they're just as good,' I told him.

Well, to cut a long story short, I agreed to sell the chap one of the dogs for £40. We arranged to meet at the "Ram Jam" the following evening, and I kept my part of the bargain and took the dog wi' me. Sure enough, he was there, we had a drink together, he handed over the £40, and I gave him the dog.

I never thought any more about it, but a few days later, I had a visit from the police. They told me they had been watching this chap and his mates for some time, as they suspected 'em of passing forged banknotes. They had just nabbed the gang red handed.'

As he neared the end of his story, Charlie became more excited. 'The police told me they were the best "forfeit" notes they had ever seen,' he blurted out, confusing "forgery" and "counterfeit" in the process.

'Did they have thin silver lines in them?' interrupted the driver's mate.

'They had every bloody thing - they were real good forfeit notes, they were,' said Charlie, emphatically. He paused, his story almost complete, drew a deep breath, and added, 'The police wanted the notes back, but I told 'em they were too late - I'd spent the beggars.' A huge grin spread across his face as he re-lived that moment of disappointment for the police. 'I've never been in the "Ram Jam" since', said Charlie.

Charlie's son, Bob, worked in the store cattle auction as a drover, so the following day I asked Bob what they did with items like the lawnmower handles.

'Simple,' said Bob, 'We get a pile and sell it as scrap. We pick up the odd Dinky toy, too - we can always sell them. Every little helps, you know.'

As with many towns throughout the country, Melton eventually clogged up with traffic. The usual debates ensued with two types of alleviating road schemes put forward. Do we have a by-pass or do we have an inner relief road? Eventually, we had to make do with the latter, and so swathes of buildings were demolished to make way for the new scheme. The ideal route for a relief road would have been on the course of the now defunct L.N.E.R. railway line, which ran on top of an embankment around the town and connected all the major roads into the town. If the embankment had been removed, as it had been at the rear of the cattle market, there would have been ample room for a wide road. However, this opportunity was lost, some years previously, when a supermarket was built on the site of the former railway station.

Unfortunately, the office and saleroom of Shouler and Son were situated right in the centre of the course of the proposed new road, and so the partners were forced to negotiate a lease on alternative office premises in Nottingham Street, to which we moved shortly after.

One morning, as I drove to work, I noticed clouds of dust billowing upwards from the interior of the former mart. I was saddened, and a strong feeling of nostalgia engulfed me. I had to see the old place once more before it was lost forever. I parked the car and walked back to see the demolition in progress. Only the outer walls remained, and they were rapidly diminishing in height as the giant, clawed, bucket pulled huge chunks of the walls inwards. The huge yellow devil, with his long jib outstretched, was standing right on the spot where, years before, I had tentatively mounted the steps to the rostrum, gavel clutched tightly in one hand, to face an audience and sell my first lot in the furniture sale.

Sadly, I bent down to pick up a couple of bricks to keep as a memento of the old office and mart. With my hand, I brushed away the dust from one of the bricks. Imprinted on the heavy brick, I could read "LION BRICKWORKS, SCALFORD, MELTON MOWBRAY" - a brickyard, five miles from town, which had been derelict for decades, but was the very place where my father was working as a kiln hand at the time of my birth.

Now, whenever I walk into town, and have to wait at the traffic lights before crossing the road at the Scalford Road junction, I think to myself, 'This is where it all began - right here - before traffic lights and yellow lines - this is where I leant my bicycle against the office wall, safe in the knowledge that it would still be there when I came out again at lunchtime.'

CHAPTER FOURTEEN

Articled students

Articled students got ten bob
For working whilst they learnt the job.
Geoff was quick to work things out,
Whilst Nigel thought he'd get a clout !
A Bentley brought a touch of class,
And Trevor didn't need a glass !

During the course of my forty seven years at Shouler &
Son there was a succession of articled students. There was
only one at any given time and he was always articled to
the senior partner, Arthur Shouler. The student was paid
a wage of ten shillings a week for "clerical assistance",
but his parents had to provide for his upkeep. During his
time with the firm he would gain practical experience
whilst studying for his professional qualifications. Some
left before taking final exams and only three stayed with
the firm after qualifying. Norman Fowler, David Willars
and Simon Allam all became partners in the firm.
Norman eventually became the senior partner.

The student at the time I joined the firm was John Sail
who left to start his National Service two weeks before
I left for my two years' service. Ironically, he started at
the same camp as I did. We did meet up once there, but

1 5 5

recruits only stayed there for two weeks before moving on to another camp and I saw him no more.

John took his demobilisation in the far east and did not return to England. Instead, he moved on and settled in Australia, taking a job on a cattle farm. Eventually, I understand, the farmer willed the farm to John and he became a successful farmer in his own right.

Another student was Geoff Wade, son of a farmer from Sedgebrook, near Grantham. Geoff was outstanding at mental arithmetic and would often astound Arthur Shouler by firing off answers to questions which most people would need to write down before working out. Sadly, Geoff, who lived in lodgings in Sandy Lane at the time, never completed his studies. He decided the profession was not for him, returned home, and eventually took over the running of the family farm.

Another student was Nigel who hailed from a wealthy background. On his first day at the office Len Hewes told him to bring in his National Insurance card, upon which Nigel replied, "You will need to speak to my solicitor about that."

Len blew a fuse and told Nigel what he could do with his solicitor. Poor Nigel was rather taken aback as this was probably his first foray into the working environment. Each student sat at the same small table as his predecessor in the control room, but Nigel complained about sitting with his back to the door. He was afraid someone would enter the room and hit him over the head with a blunt instrument. He could also spin a few tall stories about tropical fish, which he kept as a hobby, so when he persisted that he was often driven around in a chauffeur driven Bentley, there was a certain air of disbelief around the office. Much to our surprise, the next morning a large black Bentley arrived at the office and a uniformed chauffeur opened the passenger door and out stepped Nigel.

In the cattle market Nigel assisted in the rearing calf auction on Tuesdays. He had to withstand a lot of ribbing from farmers because he insisted upon wearing a pair of rubber gloves whilst handling calves. Apparently he suffered from dermatitis and used gloves as a precaution.

Another student was Trevor Vennett-Smith. I recall Trevor being very much in love with cricket. He played regularly whilst a student and for many years after he left the firm. Eventually, he set up his own successful business as an auctioneer and valuer. My lasting recollection of Trevor was the great time he had at the Christmas party, which was held at a village pub. We all had a good time and Trevor, who stayed the night at the pub, was last observed crawling along the corridor towards the toilet clutching a bottle of port. The next day he had a terrible hangover.

Shouler & Son are still thriving in Melton Mowbray, and have moved into a new, image conscious, era far removed from my years with the firm. Martin is still with the firm. One of Martin's sons, Ben, has also joined the firm, and has appeared as an auctioneer in the BBC programme, "Cash in the Attic." Martin's other son, Chris, runs the family farm at Scalford.

In a firm with such diverse interests there are stories to be told almost every day. Whether it be in the cattle market, furniture sale, on the farm, or even in the office, something surprising is about to happen.

Lightning Source UK Ltd.
Milton Keynes UK
UKOW041458091112

201934UK00001B/10/P